Sadie's Pearls

Timeless Lessons Worth Living

TINA SERPICO

with Anne Marie Merz

Dedicated to my six beautiful daughters

TINA SERPICO

Contents

Foreword

Tina desperately wants to write the book about Sadie, a truly remarkable woman whose stories and wisdom she holds deep inside as well as in her many spiral notebooks; she just needs some help getting her stories into book form.

She brings the notebooks this year when she comes for a visit from New York. At the time, I'm working as the office administrator for my oldest sister in the alluring world of music entertainment near Hollywood, California. Don't get jealous, the glamour and travel are my sister Susan's job. Me? I spend most days in front of an office computer doing accounting and so much more, but that's entirely another story.

Helping my mom began with a gift for my mother-in-law Marge. A lovely woman, who was around eighty-years-young when I created a four-hundred-picture montage playing to twenty-five songs covering over three decades of the lives of her nine children. I nearly lost it with the continual "ch-ch" sound that came with scanning a thousand forty-year-old slides, but it was well worth it to see such joy in her eyes.

Marge was touched and amazed, as was everyone who watched her family DVD, including Susan—who figured, and of course—Mom concurred: "Anne Marie is the perfect one to help you tell Sadie's story to the masses. Not only does she have a college degree, I know she can do it!"

If you knew the persuasive capacities of Susan and our sweet mom Tina, you wouldn't ask how I was finally convinced to help her write the book—clearly they were paying me a compliment—trying to send a blessing my way and I would be crazy to turn down their offer. And when I try to remind them my degree is in business, and not writing, it doesn't seem to matter.

Anne Marie Merz

PART I

⤳ Tina on the stoop ⟿
Brooklyn, New York - 1940s

CHAPTER 1

The Day I Met Sadie

I'm sweet Tina, getting ready to embark on a new chapter in my life, when for reasons unbeknownst to me, my little Italian family moves from Hegeman Avenue in one Jewish suburb of Brooklyn to Ralph Avenue, a more upscale part of the immigrant neighborhood, where I notice my fair skin and blondish hair are still not a typical sight to see.

It's the summer of 1941. I'm quite the impressionable young teenager excited about entering high school, having always been a good student, particularly interested in history, and an avid reader. Anxious to join the ranks at Samuel J. Tilden High, I convince my sister (who'll be a sophomore this year) to walk what will be our new daily route. Mary doesn't share my enthusiasm with classes not starting for at least a month, but makes the best of it, both of us laughing and chatting about this or that as we walk along. I realize we're across the street from the school only minutes later, and then take notice of two girls relaxing on a nearby stoop (a popular, cherished East Coast pastime) and they smile at us.

Determined to say more than, "Hi, I'm Tina," I ask where the nearest movie theater is located. Besides my love of books, I'm also a habitual moviegoer and go to the movies practically every Saturday. One of the girls says they love to go to the Saturday matinees at the Avenue D Theater. I wonder why I haven't seen them before today, we're all about the same age and go to the same movie theater; yet here we are, four teenage Italian-American girls meeting for the very first time.

It's odd how most New Yorkers whether young or old, stay so close to home and each other, they never seem to go beyond their own neighborhoods. It's easy to live in an area only three or four blocks wide and truly exist in your own little world—the same, yet seemingly worlds apart from everyone else.

School finally arrives, and I discover one of the girls from the stoop sitting right in front of me in history class. I'm happy when Carmela turns around, gorgeous hazel eyes smiling at me, and intrigued when she says that she has three older brothers, and not one, but four sisters. I seriously cannot fathom that many people living under the same roof, especially when my only other sibling besides Mary is little Jean, making our household of five seem quite small by comparison.

Pleasantly surprised when Carmela turns around again (this time at the end of class), to invite me to her house after school. Curiosity gets the best of me, so I say yes, and venture in. Mary decides she'll definitely join me and shares her thought that we're about to meet *The Old Woman Who Lived in the Shoe*. I imagine a woman heavily burdened by the weight of her brood, possibly smelling of onions and spices from the evening meal she's preparing. After the short walk across the street, Carmela introduces us to her brother Sonny standing in front of her house, but I take notice of a cute boy relaxing near the side door. I'm taken aback as a strikingly beautiful woman appears wearing a gorgeous Mandarin-style paisley dress and fashionable high heels. Her coiffed, jet-black wavy hair frames her beautiful face like a halo shining perfectly in the afternoon sun.

She's absolutely stunning. I'm completely floored.

My mouth stays open as she welcomes us inside with a quick wave and a bright smile. All of us girls are having a fun time hanging around the kitchen table where she serves us cups of coffee and delicious Italian cookies. I'm shocked when she joins us at the table with her cup, but when she participates in our conversation, she quickly becomes the most interesting person in the room, making me and every-one else hang on her every word; I'm enthralled.

I want to know everything I can about her.

Perhaps sensing my interest, she begins sharing her life story, right then and there, by telling us that she was born a first-generation Italian-American in Brooklyn, New York; the year was 1899 and her parents named her Assunta Tepedino. She grew up in a working-class family and her mother ran the family-owned Italian deli right from their living room. Customers literally came through the front door to shop, and her big family lived in the rest of the house. She quietly mentions this was much easier for her mother with a sickly husband at home to tend to, and this is probably why her mom depended on her children so much when it came to running the store.

As a child, she could often be found in the back of the store, reading or studying, until she was called up to the front to help with customers. She loved school so much, she would run right back after the lunch rush, "Even for just an hour more," she'd happily say, "just for the chance to learn."

I'm thrilled she was excited about school the same way I am. My favorite subject is history, hers was math, and she often dreamed of becoming a teacher.

I want to be a writer.

We laugh and talk together as the afternoon melts away much sooner than I want it to. I can't think of any other person I've ever met with whom I have more in common, and if I was originally floored by her looks, I'm leveled by our immediate connection and hope she feels the same way. To keep our conversation going, I ask if she was ever teased with such an unusual first name. "Oh no," she replies, "When I was in the first grade, my teacher may have been unaware Susan was the common English translation for the name Assunta and began calling me Sadie. After that the name just stuck."

Here I am, a shy fourteen-year-old girl getting to spend my time with this fascinating and stylish forty-two-year-old mother of eight, absolutely captivated by everything that is her home. I start to think I am in the middle of a group of friends.

I become convinced when she tells me to call her Sadie!

Sadie ~ Doesn't she look swell

CHAPTER 2

Sadie, Classy Lady

It may seem odd, given the perfectly good breakfast prepared at my house every morning that I decide to make a daily habit of rushing over to Carmela's house before school for warm biscuits, delicious coffee, and a chance to spend as much time as I possibly can with Sadie.

Our first meeting is still on my mind and I can't stop thinking of the contagious joyfulness that is her home. My life is serene, and at times, kind of dull as the middle child of three quiet girls in a house managed well by my mom and dad, so I guess I'm drawn to the fun and excitement going on over there.

Besides, my mom is the complete opposite of Sadie in style as well as daily manner. She tends to be solemn, mostly due to her mom's death at an early age, leaving her, the oldest daughter, responsible for the care of her nine brothers and sisters. My mom had to quit school at the age of nine, at first to work in the factory to help with financial responsibilities, and then to stay at home to raise her younger siblings.

Personifying the typical mother of the day, my mom goes above and beyond when it comes to keeping things tidy, and our family looking good, clean, and well fed. But you won't find her dolling up her looks or hanging around the table with a bunch of teenage girls. Don't get me wrong, she is a devoted mother and loves us very much, but she tends to do what's natural. This makes her seem much older than her years, yet I suppose it's easier to wear a housedress than a fashionable outfit and easier still to wear sensible shoes, plus my mom wouldn't even consider giving lipstick a chance.

On the other hand, Sadie wears high-heel shoes, fancy jewelry, Sweet Chantilly perfume, and makeup regularly. I love to watch Sadie use her pinky finger to apply lipstick, even when the color hasn't worn off yet, and regardless whether she has someplace special to go. When Sadie was pregnant with her first child and didn't want to look like she was with child, she persuaded her sister Katie to make a pleated blouse to distract attention away from her growing belly. I imagine her looking so stylish in that new outfit, and she had no idea she might've designed the first maternity-top, long before any modern-day fashion designer.

Relaxing in the kitchen at the very table where Sadie serves her family, I see a woman who exudes happiness as she tells yet another fascinating story.

She mesmerizes me.

It's no longer about what she wears or how she looks, and though I believe all moms exist to make other people happy, Sadie goes a step further by including herself in the joy. I saw it the first day we met, where instead of working around the house, tidying up or something, she chooses to sit with us girls, laughing and joking without missing a beat.

One particular morning my arrival is bright and early, so Sadie shares a tale about a wealthy Jewish neighbor who wanted to pay for her to go to a private high school. He admires her strong desire to learn, and his daughter isn't interested in the further education he's offering. Sadly, the man's desire for Sadie is only wishful thinking. The responsibilities to her mother make it impossible for her to go to high school, but I can tell this never discouraged Sadie from searching for knowledge wherever she can find it.

Several years before I met the family, Sadie's mother passed away, yet the way she speaks fondly of her and the lessons she taught, it makes me feel as if I know the woman who so deeply influenced Sadie's life. She shares her personal stories freely, but I get the distinct impression she has surpassed her mom by the way she tells her stories so eloquently—a little bit of Mother Carmela—and a whole lot of my new friend Sadie.

Each morning is a new adventure that engages us thoroughly as she shares thoughts about life, history, the arts, and her strong desire to travel around the world someday. When you describe someone as classy, the first thing that may come to mind is how they dress, or how they know instinctively which fork to use at a formal dinner party. These can be distinct signs of a person with class, but there's much more to the definition and she demonstrates this by the way she treats people equally, never passes judgment, and proves being classy is not about being fashionable or sociable; it arises from exceptional character—and in the eyes of anyone who meets her—Sadie is class-personified.

Every day since our first meeting justifies my initial thoughts by the way she speaks of modern, relevant things, and delivers them in such a way that is thoroughly enjoyable. Just listening to Sadie tell these stories is worth getting up early and the risk of being late for school, much like today, as Carmela and I each grab one last warm biscuit and bid our quick goodbyes.

CHAPTER 3

Enduring Faith

It's a typical Sunday afternoon in December.

Sadie's oldest daughter and I just finished watching a funny movie at our local movie theater. Theresa and I are strolling down the street pleasantly lost in conversation when someone abruptly stops us and frantically says the Japanese have bombed Pearl Harbor. It's December 7, 1941, and the state of Hawaii has been attacked.

World War II has found us—found Brooklyn.

It's surreal. In an instant, fear removes the joy of the day and firmly holds us in its grasp. Soon afterwards, America commits its resources and many young men go off to fight for our freedoms. Among them are Sadie's sons, Sonny, Jimmie, and Anthony who enlist in the Marines. On their behalf, Sadie and I, and a few of her daughters, attend church on Tuesday nights for the duration of the war to make novenas; prayers repeated many times over in hopes of obtaining intercessory graces.

Raised Catholic, I am very familiar with the church's many traditions—baptism, communion, confirmation, and of course, confession. I go to church with my family for holidays, weddings, and sometimes funerals, taking what I need and unknowingly leaving the rest. This is not the case with Sadie. Her presence at the altar each week is important, and since her son Jimmie is now my boyfriend, it must be important to me too.

One Tuesday night, we're standing at the corner of Beverly and 59th Street eagerly awaiting the Avenue D bus, but it doesn't arrive. It's getting late, and perceptibly colder by the second, so we start walking the fourteen blocks to the church hoping we'll be lucky enough catch the bus at the next stop. Before long, as if wanting to make our journey a little easier, Sadie shares this powerful story:

"I was a young woman working in the factory before I was married, heading down the stairwell toward the gleaming exit doors when two strange men step out of nowhere and grab me. I immediately began to pray out loud, in Italian, resisting them as best I could. In the midst of the struggle one of my attackers blurts out, 'Where is this girl getting her strength?' Upon hearing the fear in his voice, I prayed on, even more loudly than before."

Sadie pauses. Anna and I stop in the middle of the sidewalk to focus intently on her voice. "Somehow I managed to fight them off and ran out the door, only later did I realize God had sent an angel to protect me from great evil that night."

By this time, American forces are heavily entrenched in the war, and I'm thankful for the service men fighting for freedom, but I'm more thankful that our country is not experiencing firsthand the destruction wreaking havoc in cities across Europe and parts of the South Pacific. But I'm disappointed when I start to hear people complain about the rationing of sugar and coffee.

I wonder if they understand the sacrifices some of our servicemen will make, and of those lucky enough to return home, many will return with physical and psychological disabilities. I receive letters from Jimmie practically once a week, they help assure me he's still doing okay—until the day they stop coming. It happens in the third year. Over a month goes by without any word, until the day the radio announcer reports that the Third Marine Division, to which Jimmie is assigned, has stormed the beaches of Iwo Jima.

My heart stops.

I take a deep breath. Then I make the mad dash to see Sadie, not knowing what she'll say or whether she'll be able to alleviate my mounting fears. She gladly offers to call the Marine Corps headquarters in Virginia to find out if Jimmie is safe. We later find out that he was in the middle of the battle, but he's okay. I breathe a sustainable sigh of relief. Sadie believed in his safety all along and probably only made the call for my comfort, because Sadie's faith is miraculously unwavering.

As the war rages on, we continue to write letters and send care packages to Sadie's sons. Jimmie writes how it was a real highlight for the guys in the barracks when the salami, cheeses, and fancy Italian cookies arrived. To our great delight, every soldier wanted a taste.

What else makes this experience easier is recalling Sadie's important message from our walk that bitter cold Tuesday night. It's the same answer to her attacker's question, "Where is this girl getting her strength?"

Sadie's strength comes from having faith, and with it, trusts the angels are watching over our men. Were it not for the time I spend listening to her strong convictions and my darling Jimmie's love letters, I don't think I'll make it through.

After all, I'm a teenager deeply in love.

Sadie is rewarded the day she learns from his latest letter that her three sons recently met up on Iwo Jima. It's beyond coincidence to her, and she believes they will all be home soon. Only a few months later, Sonny and Jimmie indeed return home, safe and sound. Jimmie and I are eager to get married, but Sadie asks us to wait until after Anthony returns home.

So Jimmie and I wait.

I'm sharing this chapter with you early in the book, because there is no understanding Sadie without it. And I learned Sadie's lesson that warm, sunny morning firsthand. You must continue to have strong faith despite life's many difficulties, and that is why over time, as my admiration for Sadie grows, so do my own beliefs.

I'm a good catholic getting better.

Sadie is a very good catholic.

─◌ **Tina and Sadie** ◌─
Celebrating Easter Sunday during WWII

The Early Years

BY ANNE MARIE

I often find myself saying, "Is it coincidence that seems to make everything work out just right in the end, or is it fate?"

Mom emphatically replies, "No Anne Marie, it is God." She truly adheres to the belief that life leads you in ways you cannot fathom on your own and her replies invariably include, "It's okay if we're sidetracked, because it will work out as it is supposed to," and the not so reassuring, "Don't worry, it's all part of the plan." I question this point of view and she knows it, but she'll definitely try to justify our delayed start, yet again.

Another day, another pleasant delay, but this day is passing one o'clock already and we've had the leisurely breakfast and the post-breakfast chat. After my quick clean up in the kitchen, I find Mom in the guest room, on the phone talking finances with my sister Jeanne, and she's still not ready to work.

So I'm forced to go at it alone.

I head into my home office, pick up Mom's worn spiral notebook where she's been compiling Sadie's many lessons and detailed stories for at least ten years. As I flip through the pages for a good place to start, I notice few messages have titles and though many pages start out neat, not a single one ends that way. To make matters worse, it'll be a grand task, in and of itself, to decipher her chicken-scratch handwriting style.

I finally decide upon a fairly legible page (despite its lack of a title) and turn the page to get a better idea where the lesson is going. To my joyful surprise, it's a story from my mom's early days with Sadie, the very one she talked about during our leisurely teatime this morning.

Maybe we are working, after all, but I don't dare tell her.

PART II

Tina with Jimmie on furlough – Love Birds

CHAPTER 4

Captivating Traditions

As far back as I can remember I've always wanted more out of life—more love, more affection, more warmth, and yes, more loudness. I feel like all of this came to me the day I met Sadie.

Sadie epitomizes the expression, "The mother is the heart of the home," and this is no truer than on a holiday such as Mother's Day. The day we celebrate moms everywhere with a customary breakfast in bed, handmade card, and for many, a bouquet of flowers. But when my friend Carmela invites me to spend the afternoon with their family on Mother's Day, I accept for two reasons. First, I'll have plenty of time to be with my mom in the morning, and secondly, based upon my fabulous experience last New Year's Eve, I'm too excited to miss it.

This was the New Year's Eve after I met Sadie, and knowing how enthralled I've become with this woman, you can only imagine my joy to welcome in 1942 with Sadie and both of our families. Following delicious appetizers, a fabulous meal, coffee and yummy cakes for dessert, I'm surprised as she passes around another full plate of food as the New Year arrives.

How do you enhance a tradition?

If you're Sadie, you do more than what is expected. If you're Sadie, you want everyone to feel the specialness of the moment and to celebrate the stroke of midnight with a Jewish tradition meant to bring good fortune to one and all, all year long. Anticipating another irresistible treat made by Sadie's hands, I'm puzzled to see its pieces of pickled herring as she walks quickly about the room making sure each one of us taste the strong, oily fish. To the hesitant guests, (and there are many among us) she gently nudges, "Even if it's a morsel."

I oblige, and for the record, it's terrible—terribly fun.

These moments along with the countless number of holidays, birthdays, and anniversaries we celebrate each year are the bookmarks of people's lives. Every family has their own way to observe the birth of a child, the wedding of a family member, or the ultimate passing of a loved one, and we are no exception. Sadie and I had passed one year as friends when I attend my first "Sadie's Mother's Day" party. I arrive early, peek through the side door and see Sadie is already sitting down center stage at the dining room table. I rush in the side door and take the last available seat, just to get as close as I can to Sadie.

She is the center of attention, wearing a soft-red flowy dress which accents her dark shoulder-length curls and surprisingly youthful figure. I'm close enough to see the joy in her eyes as sons and daughters make a grand procession of presenting seven white corsages. I well up with tears as

Jeanne, Sadie's adorable and youngest child, rushes up from her chair to hand her mother the last cluster of fluffy-white carnations; she doesn't hesitate to pin them on her overly-crowded apron, currently adorned with dozens of sweet-smelling flowers.

This is the woman I admire, filled with an exuberance and love for life, family, and yes, selflessness—for lo and behold—Sadie's wearing an apron, ready to finish preparing the meal, on her special day. For this reason and countless others, Sadie is a captivating tradition in her own right; one meant to be truly celebrated. The moment I enter the house, I can smell Sadie's signature dish warming in the oven, the one I've heard so much about with its oozing layers of thick pasta, marinara sauce, and rich ricotta cheese.

○ **Our Engagement Party** ○
Jimmie and Tina ~ 1945

I can't wait to try it.

I'm extra curious since my mom never cooks with ricotta cheese because Dad doesn't like the taste. I taste my first bite of Sadie's amazing lasagna, and I'm hooked, but my sudden and permanent addiction to the lasagna isn't the only reason I want Sadie to teach me how to cook. Maybe if I learn to whip up her delicious recipes, this will bring her infectious excitement into my home one day too. And if Sadie is the heart of the family, then the kitchen is the heart of her home, and I want these things in my life—just as much as I always want Sadie to be in my life.

CHAPTER 5

Why Buy the Cow?

For Jimmie and me, it's love at first sight.

I clearly recall seeing him the same day I met Sadie. Although she captured my attention standing in the doorway that sunny afternoon, the handsome young man who sat casually outside in a lawn chair caught my eye. Within three months, Jimmie and I begin keeping company. Soon afterwards, I find myself sharing everything about our budding relationship with Sadie. Jimmie may be her son, but she has fast become my girlfriend, and girlfriends talk about boys all the time.

It's an unwritten law or something.

As I express how crazy I am for Jimmie, Sadie responds, "Don't be crazy; be careful. And if Jimmie gets fresh with you, hit him over the head with a bottle." At first I laugh thinking she's just given me permission to knock out her son—who wouldn't? But based on the way Sadie looks back at me with the utmost sincerity, I decide I had better take her comment seriously.

Sadie's concerns continue to grow; she realizes it could be possible for us to get into trouble, especially since I'm only fourteen-years-old to Jimmie's eighteen-and-a-half. That's the main reason his mother places the majority of the responsibility on his shoulders, wanting him to be respectful and admonishing him to treat me the way he would want his sisters to be treated. I'm listening to everything she has to say concerning us and realize his mom hopes for something more; a meaningful relationship that will last. This makes me smile.

I too want there to be more.

Sadie makes this possible by allowing us to date in her home; the old-fashioned way. At the time I don't realize the value of this, and don't realize how much she's watching over us on a daily basis, but as time goes by, our love grows deeper and deeper. It's a wonderful thing to be able to take your time with something as special as courtship, and this leads Sadie to share more of her wisdom—this time with my father.

This is usually a conversation between men, you know, father-to-father, but Sadie doesn't observe customs the way anybody else does. When my dad becomes aware my dating Jimmie is serious, he doesn't like it, so it's a good thing she pays him a visit. Imagine Sadie going to see my dad to talk about a relationship with her son?

She explains that if he forbids me from seeing Jimmie, it would be the worst thing he could do; it would result in us sneaking around to be together.

Sadie is absolutely right.

Being forbidden to see Jimmie would've made me sneak around just to be with him, that's how much I love him. She encourages my dad to understand and support us as best he can. Because I am not there, I don't know exactly what was said, but I'm sure Sadie got her point across because things between my dad and Jimmie got better. I can tell she would like her son to make me her daughter-in-law by the way she is setting the stage for what will hopefully become the blending of our families.

I've heard detailed stories on the subject of chastity as told by Sadie's greatest admirers; she was well into her eighties when many of her great-granddaughters were taken aside to hear the lesson, when no one was talking about sex, even though there was a lot of sex happening. Sadie sharing her ideals about love might be hard to imagine at that age, but you'll have to, since she did it all the days of her life.

Naturally, for each generation the story was a little different, but it was the same Sadie, believing and teaching the same thing, never letting her age or the age of the listener stop her. Sadie's look was softened by reddish-golden hair and pinkish lipstick by the time Christi Anne received her Sadie-stamped lesson on the subject. Imagine our dear Sadie saying to her in a sweet aged voice, "Why buy the cow, if you can get the milk for free?" Christi Anne recalls the day Grandma Sadie, whose striking stature had diminished with age, sits very near to her, and leans in with a powerful touch saying, "Christi Anne, there is nothing wrong in going with a boy or getting friendly, and if he gets friendly and places one hand on your leg and the other hand on your shoulder, that's perfectly fine."

Sadie demonstrates the first gesture by laying her warm, crippled hand onto Christi Anne's knee, "But if his hand goes up any further, you let him know that's not where his hand belongs."

Sadie emphasizes abstinence before marriage at all times, which is advice Jimmie and I gladly followed. Fortunately, her directive to hit a boy over the head with a bottle is a long-gone adage, but her message on the virtue of chastity is clear: abstinence matters. Sadie's message came to each of them as it did to me, in the way they needed to hear it.

CHAPTER 6

One, Two, Cha-Cha-Cha

It's the mid-1950s and dancing the *Cha-Cha* is all the rage with its lively music, and fancy Latin moves. I mention the dance class I want to attend at Tilden High to Sadie, and to my delightful surprise, she wants to join me. I'm a young mother excited about the chance to get out of the house for a few hours, so the next day, my sister, Mary, and several of her daughters go with us to sign up; setting out to go faithfully every Tuesday night.

The minute class begins, Sadie instantly lays claim as the best dancer in the class. It's no surprise she fits right in with a dance that starts on the fourth beat with a "one, two, cha-cha-cha," as she takes the distinctive one step forward and two steps back. Practically thirty years older than anyone in the class, and yet she appears to be born for the energetic, steady beat pulsating throughout our old school gymnasium.

Who knew Sadie could be so great at a dance that required a leader and a follower—and she would be the one following?

I stand in awe watching her on the dance floor because in life Sadie always seems to take the lead. I've been around the family long enough to see her accustomed to giving direction, as she is so often asked to do; family and friends look to her for answers when things in life are questionable or uncertain.

I believe her ever-positive outlook and adventurous spirit have much to do with it. Sadie enjoys a modern life and goes after it in many positive ways. Her very presence in our dance class speaks to that fact. We have a lot of fun trying to learn the dance, but for me, six months in and it still feels like Sadie and I are the only ones on the dance floor, save for our partners, young men who dip and twirl us while having eyes only for her.

Never shy to take a compliment, yet she's quick to remind them they're around the same age as her sons. Nevertheless, her joyful spirit keeps them coming back for more, as do the fancy dresses she wears on dance night, impressing all of us. Sadie's decision to learn the *Cha-Cha* says a lot about her philosophy on life too, believing you never stop living, learning, or dancing, for however long your song plays. Dancing makes everyone feel young, and it helps you discover who you are. When you dance nothing defines you, not even age.

I thought Sadie saying yes to the dance class was terrific, but it was her saying yes to the rhythmic moves of the Cha-Cha that is an amazing testament to dancing to your own beat!

She is without a doubt an adventure taker, and once we master the moves of the *Cha-Cha,* we're off to Monday night at the movies, which fast becomes our newest weekly adventure. Not that we ever need a reason to go the movies, and we don't choose Monday nights as an excuse to socialize on a weekday. Instead, it's Sadie who informs us that on Monday nights the Avenue D Theater is giving away a piece of dinnerware with your admission ticket— and the added promise of a sparkling set of dishes doesn't hurt anyone.

All us young mothers sign up with Sadie, and by the end of fifty-two weeks of romance, comedy, and dramas, we've had a real blast. Plus, we each collect a lovely eight-piece set of dishes, complete with sugar bowl, creamer, and a nice platter. Between us, there are enough butter dishes for a small army, we almost grow weary of the stretch of weeks where butter dishes are the only available piece, but we tough it out.

My mom rarely goes anywhere without my dad and probably wouldn't go to the movies for a new set of dinnerware (no matter how much fun it might be). She thinks it's easier to buy dishes, besides she wouldn't want the same set as everyone else in the neighborhood. Those matching sets came in handy when Carmela, Jeanne and I needed to share dishes or platters for our larger and larger family gatherings. The other reason I choose to do fun things with Sadie and not my mom is because our relationship as mother and daughter is totally different than the cherished friendship which exists between Sadie and me.

Mom realizes Sadie is that special someone in my life, much like a favorite aunt, my Aunt Fanny comes to mind (or a terrific teacher I can be proud to emulate) and isn't at all jealous of our budding friendship; she understands why it always has to be—Sadie and me.

Together, we're two *social* peas in a pod.

⌒ **Sadie and Tina** ⌒

Two social peas in a pod

Working Vacations

BY ANNE MARIE

Quite a few of my revelations impress Mom so much, that lately we find ourselves repeating her overused comment to each other—good enough for government work—as we confidently move on to our next topic. My mom says she wants to pay me for my time, but I can't take her money, so this is definitely not government work.

"I'll pay you some day, Anne Marie," she politely chimes in a moment later, "especially if we strike it rich with Oprah's Book Club, or perhaps, Doubleday."

I have my doubts.

Many of our co-writing challenges are due to our bi-coastal living situation. Mom lives in the lovely quaint town of Millbrook, New York, and I live in the sunny city of Mission Hills, California, over three thousand miles away. Though she visits us for at least a few months every winter, Mom has such a long list of family and friends to visit when she is here, I hardly see her sometimes.

In case you're wondering, she can barely figure out how to work her DVD player, let alone a computer, so Skype is out of the question. And I can't finish writing Sadie's story without her, regardless of the grand optimism she's always trying to sell me; I need her input and deciphering skills. There's good news however, some days we both get a good laugh out of her failed attempts to make heads or tails of that chicken-scratch writing style, and it's not only me. "Life has many challenges," she reminds me again, "but when we follow our lifelong dreams with steadfast conviction, Anne Marie, it will often lead to great success."

By challenges, she means not working on the book despite promises to mark her calendar for work, and not social events. Following our daily routine of morning coffee, breakfast, and the post-breakfast chat, we finally find ourselves in the home office making headway on the book. We're feeling pretty good with our efforts and decide to take a break. It's around four in the afternoon, but right after we sit down at the tiny table (the one with a bird's-eye view of the front door) my husband strolls in, and finds us not working, once again.

Instead, we're enjoying a cup of tea.

Mom is usually the one defending us, though I keep telling her Paul doesn't mind me helping write the book, yet I find myself defending us today. "We really were just working!" But he doesn't believe either one of us these days. Who would with a load full of her teacups in the dishwasher from just one day's adventures? Her Sadie-like optimism has obviously sucked me in, regardless of the personal revelations that are hitting me hard. I must stick this out regardless how long it takes us to finish, for Mom's sake.

PART III

Our Wedding Day ~ June 8, 1946

Love birds married at last . . .

CHAPTER 7

'Cause You Can't Eat Bricks

I spend most days hanging out at Sadie's house; I can't seem to get enough of that woman with her clever advice, and pleasant boisterous family.

Wanting to be around her is probably more in response to what's going on in my daily life. I'm worried about my pending marriage to Jimmie, and I'm not sure what to do with regard to running a household. At eighteen, I possess no cooking, cleaning, or financial skills, which seems like a real surprise to everyone, but Mom has such a great way of taking care of us, I never had to worry.

Like most of the mothers these days, mine doesn't work. She dedicates her time to our father and is perfection when it comes to taking care of me, my two sisters, and all of our needs. I spent many pleasant days with her teaching me how to sew scarfs and dresses from beautiful fabrics. These are cherished memories along with those of us girls playing quietly in the living room, eagerly awaiting our dad's return.

As the oldest of eleven children growing up in East New York, my mom learned to keep house at an early age (after her mother passes away). Instead of having a carefree lifestyle, she spent her youth caring for many siblings. Perhaps many would say this created a harsh life for a young girl, but looking on the bright side, it prepared her exceedingly well for marriage, and for motherhood. I can only explain my lack of ability by the fact that she wants her children to enjoy life in ways she wasn't able to, even if this means our ability to be financially savvy or self-sufficient is lacking. For me, finding time to read was how I most enjoyed life. Books, whether mine or someone else's, are a treasured joy, far more important than learning to make spaghetti sauce or how to wash the clothes properly.

Mom believes I will be a famous writer someday; I love school and writing that much. As a child, I spent much of my spare time reading books or writing stories and could be found sitting in my room stapling together the pages of my newest tale until I was practically dragged away for dinner. My sister Mary was a musical prodigy, so my mom and dad took her to Manhattan for singing and piano lessons. Indulging your children in the arts this way is practically unheard of among the Italians around here, but she wants us to experience new things and to enjoy our lives, thus I'm truly at a loss.

Nevertheless, the big day arrives.

It's June 8, 1946 and I finally marry my precious Jimmie!

The ceremony goes off without a hitch, followed by a fine wedding reception at the Imperial Hall.

There is no registry or large table waiting to place your gifts. Italians don't give gifts; they give envelopes containing joyful sentiments, and money. Jimmie and I greet relatives and friends as they wait in the long reception line to congratulate us on their way into the hall. We promptly hand the envelopes over to Sadie; the guests may give us three dollars here and occasionally a ten there, but if we're lucky, a few of those crisp-white envelopes will contain twenty-dollar bills along with their well-wishes.

Sadie is not only the mother of the groom; she garners the special honor of holding the money bag at our reception. Perched behind the dais that is the focal point of the room, the money bag lies safely across her lap as over a hundred smiling Italians swirl in front of her on the packed dance floor. Everyone looks overjoyed, especially Jimmie and me; love birds married at last.

Several guests go the dais to offer Sadie their congratulatory wishes and present their cards, she smiles brightly while placing their envelopes into the overstuffed bag. From my vantage point, center of the dance floor; this looks like it could be a scene right out of a gangster movie with "Mother Sadie" ever the fashionista wearing a magnificent black-chiffon dress and holding on dearly to what will be our family treasure.

After the festivities end, Jimmie and I decide to get a place of our own. Apartment shortages force many newlyweds to live with their parents, and we're no exception. Granted, living at home for the time being does relieve my household worries, but when my sister Mary falls for

Sonny, Sadie's oldest son, and they get married, we're all living together at my parents. Two additional occupants are due to arrive; and on August 24th (only one week after their daughter Mary Ann is born), I give birth to a healthy baby girl. Jimmie and I name her Susan, to honor Sadie.

The housing shortages still make it practically impossible to get a place, but I want my budding family to have their own home, and I'm determined to make it happen. I find an apartment where I can pay an extra five-hundred-dollar fee in order to move in. This is a lot of money (five-hundred dollars back then had the same buying power as five-thousand today), but I'm pretty desperate.

Mom completely understands why we want our own place, gives her blessing, and may want to give me financial advice, but she cannot teach me the financial lessons that Sadie can. I mention my plan to rent the apartment to Sadie, before paying the extra money. She strongly suggests we consider buying a house, instead of renting.

"First off," she says, "Jimmie's salary is nowhere near the amount of money your folks see every month, so you'll have to change your lifestyle to do it. And if you're going to get ahead, you'll also have to make an effort to live on the money Jimmie brings home each week and you'll need a little savings, so try to put away some money each week, even if it's only two dollars."

I wonder if Sadie's plan is out of reach.

Could Jimmie and I really afford to buy our own house?

I'm not knowledgeable about finances and I don't know what we should do. Maybe sensing my trepidation, Sadie shares more of her thoughts: "Tina, why put your hard-earned savings and Jimmie's salary toward rent every month if you don't have to? Put it toward something that'll work for you instead. Here's what you'll do; you can take the five hundred you saved from living with your parents and add it to the fifteen hundred dollars from your wedding, and use the money as a down payment for a house. You'll be able to do it."

I'll be able to do it!

I trust Sadie, so I scrap my original plan and head out to look at houses. I find a lovely three-story brick one right across the street from a schoolyard in a nice part of Brooklyn. It's the first house on the block, near the corner of Farragut Road and East 42nd Street, and it has room for my growing family with two additional floors for renters, which can help us pay the higher mortgage payment than I had anticipated.

We can afford this beautiful Calder's House and it is exactly what Sadie said to look for—something that'll work for you.

However, to finalize the deal, I discover we need an additional five hundred dollars for closing costs. Sadie believes in us, and our future, and wastes no time in asking her sister Katie (who still runs the family business) to lend us the money. This thoughtful gesture helps us buy the house we love, and Sadie helps us stay on track by showing me how to shop for bargains, reminding me to check for things on sale. I often find myself traveling from one local supermarket to the next sometimes, barely saving a dollar. I wonder if it's worth the effort. Sadie assures me it's worth it and the money will add up.

And it does.

When it comes to the dreaded chore of paying monthly bills, Sadie teaches me to sort the money into envelopes to keep track of where every penny needs to go (a good practice I continue to this day). Attaching her financial flair to the simple adage, she says this, "Tina, it's not as important how much money you make each month, but how you manage the money you do have to pay your mortgage and all the bills, plus enough to feed the family—'cause you can't eat bricks."

"And Tina, remember there is value in living within your means, and though there are times you'll have to eat pasta and beans every night for a week to accomplish it (and there were times it felt like we did), what can you do?"

There are many times we sacrifice the things we want for the things we need, but our family makes the most of what we do have and thoroughly enjoy our lives. So much that some people in our neighborhood think we're rich. Sadie could often be heard saying to young mothers struggling to make ends meet, "Don't worry, with a little effort, you'll be living quite well."

Sadie's plan is working.

Jimmie and I manage to raise a happy family on her advice. We may not have been living on Wisteria Lane like the stars of Desperate Housewives, and this may not be my dream house, but it is our home. A home that works perfectly for our family and is within our budget—'cause you can't eat bricks.

And, in this day and age, you still can't.

—◌ Sadie, Jimmie, Tina and his dad, Jimmie ◌—

The Long and Winding Road

BY ANNE MARIE

Like so many stories in this book, I wasn't born yet and we're at a standstill since Mom says Sadie's frequent use of the phrase, "Money makes the blind see," is an integral part of the message we're working on this week. I can't seem to piece it together. "Isn't it a positive thing when a person is healed of blindness?"

Mom only agrees with a nod, so I ask another question. "Why is something as glorious as being healed of blindness associated with greed—one of the deadly sins?"

Neither one of us wants to answer that question, so Mom asks what I think the parable means. I say that I understand the love of money is the root of all evil and everyone should avoid it, but when I expound further upon my theories about Sadie's message, I realize I must be completely off-base because *Mom* looks completely bewildered.

"Pretty philosophical," she replies sheepishly. That's what happens when a business major takes seven college electives from the philosophy department. It turns out to be a good day of writing, nonetheless, especially after Mom suggests we call her sister-in-law, Carmela, who said, "Think of Sadie's lesson this way: 'A man cannot serve two gods.' If a blind man sees the actions of the rich man, and envies the rich man who puts the love of money above all things, and possibly to great harm—excessive wealth his primary goal—the blind man cannot change what he sees or might have become lost himself in the same pursuit."

"The blind man sees figuratively, not literally."

Wait—is it true? The parable on "Money Makes the Blind See" is shaping up and we might be moving onto the next chapter sometime this decade. Not quite yet, since Aunt Carmela has one final message, "Anne Marie, we just listened and learned and we didn't ask for explanations."

Carmela and Jeanne are extremely proud of my mom for courageously writing this book in honor of their mother. They value Sadie's unique, poignant lessons and now thanks to their sharing their personal stories and profound insights, I'm getting a glimpse of a life with Sadie.

I'm learning just by listening, just like they did.

⎯◠ **Our Wonderful Parents** ◠⎯
Jimmie, Sadie, Mary, and Anthony - 1950s

CHAPTER 8

Money Makes the Blind See

It's a day like any other as Carmela and I sit at Sadie's kitchen table drinking cups of coffee. This time we're listening to Carmela share a sad story about a friend whose grandfather has recently passed away. She knows that while the family grieves there will be many things to be taken care of, and important decisions to be made. Even though life is hard for them right now, she believes everything will work out okay in the end.

As I glance over at Sadie, I see she isn't so sure about that, as the constant twinkle in her eyes has all but dimmed. She proceeds to tell us about a personal experience which occurs in the days after her mother passed away.

It happens before the reading of her mother's will.

Sadie, who was only in her late thirties at the time, began tearing up her sister's IOUs along with all the others from friends and customers who received store credit over the years. This was done upon the explicit verbal wishes of her dying mother. Yet upon learning of her actions, one of her siblings became upset, believing that forgiving the debts was unfair, and tries to convince her to stop. Sadie could have responded by backing down, instead she stood her ground, "Excuse me, this is what our mother wanted," and she proceeded to tear up the rest of the notes, right then and there.

The lesson Sadie imparts is clear.

The love of money can reveal things about people that no one suspects, and it can often happen to the ones we least expect will fall victim to its pitfalls. So never let the love of money be your moral guide, there are far more valuable things in life. Her final thought on the subject is this, "Never leave the window open because you never know what might fly in."

In other words, let your children know your final wishes while your eyes are open, since you never want your children to fight over their inheritances. In the past few years, several of my daughter's friends told me heartbreaking stories of contested inheritances in their families. No matter what precautions were taken in planning and carrying out the wishes of the deceased, there always seems to be someone upset with the outcome.

Even when the estate is divided equally, one beneficiary may want to sell the assets while another may want to wait, or yet another may try to buy them out for a low price, and fighting invariably ensues. In one rather pertinent story, the youngest daughter was named the executor of the family trust. In the process of finalizing the distribution of the assets, two siblings decided to sue the estate and a good portion of their inheritance was spent fighting the parent's wishes. Despite reconciliation between them years later, the pain and loss of the friendship of her siblings was heartbreaking to see firsthand.

This reminds me of another story Carmela told while seated at this very table when we were young mothers, however she was speaking of much happier times.

Her grandmother Carmela runs the family grocery store long after Sadie moves her budding family to a nice Jewish suburb of Brooklyn where Sadie knows her children will receive the best possible education. Carmela begins by sharing pleasant memories of summers spent visiting her grandmother at the family farm, but if you want to be technical, the farm is still in Brooklyn.

Life is just different on the farm.

Carmela doesn't speak Italian, but has heard it spoken all of her life and must have a pretty good understanding of Italian because she understands her grandmother's odd dialect, so days spent on the farm were enjoyable. She also loved the early morning walks with her grandmother that included picking fresh vegetables from the farm. Carmela was gently directed as to which vegetables to pick and where to go to gather them. On the walk back, she proudly watched her grandmother give away vegetables to family, friends, and the people she would see selling trinkets along the way.

When they asked how much they owed, her grandmother was heard saying, "Oh, don't worry, it's in my head."

I never met Grandmother Carmela, but I suspect she received added blessings for her generosity, (thirty-fold, in fact, if you believe the Bible), since her answer, "Oh, don't worry, it's in my head" actually means you don't have to pay. This is likely why her dying wish to Sadie was to rip up every last note.

An ever gracious heart led her to forgive everyone's debt that day; it was her last chance and she took it. However, not even Grandmother Carmela ever expected her dying wishes would harm family relations.

Unfortunately, Sadie knows that for a time, it did.

CHAPTER 9

What I Lend You, I Lend You

Jimmie wants his girls to have everything without me having to worry about money, so he often works two or three jobs to support the family, and gives me his paychecks at the end of every month.

In return, I give him a modest allowance, which I carefully set aside from our budget. A man needs some personal money, and Jimmie's is placed in a small envelope resting inside the nightstand on his side of the bed. But when it turns out our family car needs replacing and the financial timing isn't great, Jimmie still mentions he wants to upgrade to the more expensive model. He's always had good taste, (something he inherited from Sadie) and one of the reasons I fell in love with him in the first place. As we consider the purchase further, I come to the conclusion we can't afford the nicer model, not out of our budget, and suggest he pick the cheaper model.

That's when Jimmie asks Sadie for a substantial loan.

Sadie says yes.

Months later while standing on Mary and Sonny's porch, Sadie asks me if I can start paying the car loan payments back out of our budget. At first, I tell her in no uncertain terms, "Don't you think you should ask Jimmie to pay the loan back out of his side money, since he's the one who wanted to buy the fancier car; the one I said we can't afford out of our budget?" And Sadie replied, "Oh Tina, that's not a fair statement. Jimmie's side money isn't very much and a car is a necessity; and since you handle the finances, if you can afford the payments, you should do it. Besides, thanks to Jimmie, the whole family is enjoying the spectacular new Cadillac."

I'm listening; aware every effort should be made to pay back any money you borrow. I've heard this message before, as Sadie reiterates the main point, "Making the payment is not only the right thing to do, it should be done regardless whether you can afford to do it easily, and at the very least, you should do your best to pay back a small amount every month."

Sadie ends with this gem, "But Tina, there can always be room for grace," believing that after five years, if someone truly can't afford to repay a debt (for whatever reason) the money can be placed in the "gifts" column. The Bible calls it the "Year of Jubilee" and as written, after fifty years, all unmet financial obligations can be forgiven. Sadie's day of Jubilee happens in the fifth year. She lets all the loans go. Generous beyond her means, her actions say it best, but so do her meaningful words, "I know forgiving the loan blessed them too."

Gifts and Loans

BY ANNE MARIE

"What I Give You, I Give You, but what I Lend You, I Lend You" may sound like a simple title, but believe me, it isn't. My mom has written at least ten stories about Gifts and Loans, but most of the loans become gifts, making it impossible to write this chapter in a way that makes any sense. That is, until I happen upon "Sadie's Five-Year-Forgive-a-Loan Plan"—a plan Mom has obviously adopted. I finally understand why most loans become gifts and have another important revelation later that night which makes everything work out splendidly.

So what may you ask happened later that night?

Mom and I are invited to Jeanne's house for a fabulous John Dreyer inspired dinner, her husband is a well-known cook in this family, and we can use a nice meal following a long day working at her apartment. As expected, dinner was delicious. Following coffee and dessert, Jeanne's daughter Christine graciously washes the dishes as the rest of us relax at their dining room table, nursing our coffee and cake. We're casually discussing Sadie's lessons when Jeanne's son abruptly stands up from his armchair at the mere mention of loans.

He begins by imitating his Grandma Tina.

In a deep and stern voice, John Michael blurts out her line, "What I give you, I give you, but what I lend you, I lend you." He shakes his finger at us repeatedly as he speaks; we laugh, and nod in agreement as he continues on with an amazingly straight face.

"John Michael, I'll loan you the eight hundred dollars from my envelope to pay the cell phone bill, but don't forget, 'what I lend you, I lend you,' and you'll definitely need to pay the money back."

John Michael has heard this lesson many times before, like me. I can tell by the way he manages his act to perfection. Earlier today, Mom told me a sweet story about her dear friend Bernice who paid back her loan, little by little, but also praised John Michael by saying how he specifically paid his loan back in one-hundred dollar increments, in exactly eight months.

John Michael got the point. Sometimes loans are just loans.

❖　❖　❖

What I Lend You, I Lend You

I find myself agreeing with Sadie regarding the car loan for the Cadillac by the end of our conversation on the porch that day. Later that night, I decide to make the appropriate financial adjustments to our budget in order to accommodate for the car payment. It isn't easy, but it feels great to do the right thing.

Yes, there is value in the money Sadie loaned Jimmie, but it's not about the money—it's about the character I develop as I take care of our debt.

To the superbly wise quote, generally attributed to Abraham Lincoln, "You can please some of the people all of the time and you can please all of the people some of the time, but you can't please all of the people, all of the time," Sadie would softly add, "no matter how much you love and respect them." Keep in mind that not everyone in your life will be happy with the choices you make for your life and they may not be happy with the suggestions you may make for their lives, so it's best to let people do what they want to do. It's their life, after all.

Sadie understands what this means.

I almost forgot about it years later over a similar issue when my daughter Marie comes to live with us after selling her house in South Florida. She loves living with us in La Grangeville and we loving having her here, but when we're straightening out finances, somewhere in our conversation I imply Marie knows she owes me the money and she should pay me back. She asks me why I'm being rude to her. I'm not trying to be rude, but Marie says my remarks make her feel as if I'm calling her cheap.

That's not what I intended, but I don't tend to yell or get verbally upset, I don't have to; my glaring eyes have a way of saying it all—so Marie was right in being hurt and upset. Sadie is much better at resolving tough situations and if ever asked how she does it, she says there's always a better way to handle your differences. My mistake was failing to use her gentle wisdom of confronting the situation, and not communicating my feelings to Marie earlier.

Sadie is a fabulous negotiator and a bona fide peacemaker.

I am still learning, and I pay for it by not being able to sleep all night. I feel awful about the situation I have created between us. The next morning, I promptly kiss Marie and sincerely apologize, being sure to let her know how truly sorry I am about what happened yesterday afternoon. We make up.

And in the case of any loan, Sadie would say, "If you cannot resolve the situation, you have three choices: You can move the loan to the gifts column, agree to disagree about the payment plan, or you can end a relationship forever." But who really wants to do the latter? Sadie doesn't. I like that about her and follow her lead.

Today is well under the five-year mark, but I forgive Marie's loan anyway. We have a heart-to-heart—and begin focusing on what matters most—being mother and daughter.

Polishing the Lessons

BY ANNE MARIE

A whole section, "On Being a Mother" isn't going to be written by me alone, regardless of whether I am happily married and a wonderful aunt to many. I'm at a severe disadvantage when it comes to polishing these lessons because not only am I the baby of the family, I have no practical experience from my teenage years (I was a hostess, not a babysitter) and haven't personally experienced the joy of raising children.

To make matters worse, the seniors in Mom's apartment complex think she's living a life of leisure—jetting coast-to-coast twice a year to California—with trips to Manhattan in between to see the latest Broadway plays—and they gossip to each other and the management about her constant travels. They don't understand she's working when she comes here. But it doesn't matter, since neither her neighbors' unfounded complaints, nor the years that have since passed have lessened her determination to finish, so Mom plans to visit us in November with a plan to head back to New York in time for Christmas with the Dreyer's.

To fill in the blanks with nostalgic visuals, Mom has brought pictures; today we're enjoying a string of oldies but goodies from Sadie's early life, but for me, three stand out in particular. One is a Polaroid of a youthful Sadie (the grandmother of the bride) wearing her signature red-velvet lipstick and a fitted emerald-green dress with bright-white bands in all the right

＿ᗣ **Celebrating Sadie's 65th Birthday** ᗣ＿

March 9, 1964

＿ᗣ **Twenty-six grandchildren and counting . . .** ᗣ＿

places—she carries it with no effort. In another, Sadie is vibrant and true to her life, with a bright smile, wearing a deep-purple sweater which compliments her thick-luscious black hair and soft complexion. She is pointing the decorative knife needed to cut her birthday cake, but it's the bracelet dangling from her left wrist that jumps out at you.

The heavy bracelet is adorned with twenty-six golden charms of elaborated-designed boy and girl silhouettes presented earlier that evening by her children as her 65th birthday present. Each golden charm is carefully engraved with the names and birth dates of her grandchildren, and Sadie wears the bracelet with such pride.

Wow, my mom is a lot like Sadie.

Tina's 80th birthday party had all of the essentials: An elegant party held at Angela's spectacular house in the canyons; a fancy feast of antipasto and piping hot lasagna; plus, a crowd of family, friends, and a television star. Tina looks radiant—and not a day over sixty-five in a modern-day black chiffon dress that compliments her golden, blondish hair and a dramatic corsage (a billowing, fragrant Gardenia), and she carries it beautifully.

The colorful sunset is being admired by many guests on the back patio overlooking the San Fernando Valley, including her friend and actor, Gavin MacLeod, when the doorbell rings and Mom is quickly summoned to the front door where she sees her grandson Vincent, his darling wife and her great-granddaughter, Marie, who have come three thousand miles to celebrate her special day. Excitement, family, and tradition surround Tina that whole night and she's still aglow days after the big event.

My 80th Birthday Celebration
Gavin MacLeod and Tina

The additional mothering I'm receiving, plus the extensive learning that has met us both equally during this process has been nothing short of a miracle. I sense our time together will pass all too quickly as her social schedule is bound to get the best of us, especially after hearing my mom accept invitations from excited party guests.

I'm astonished how Sadie's lessons are passed on when you least expect them, and sometimes in the oddest ways. One such incident occurred at my local deli counter when I mention to the clerk about the medicine my husband takes to lower his blood pressure, and the low-sodium turkey he eats to help with the cause. The clerk mentions a plant extract which acts as a natural alternative to lower high blood pressure that he could try. As a joke, I ask, "Do cocktails help?"

The clerk surprisingly answers, "When Scotch breaks down in the body the alcohol can be an effective natural cure for high blood pressure, similar to the plant extract I was mentioning." Sadie rarely drank alcohol, though she did enjoy the occasional beer with a slice of pizza, and as Sadie would aptly and adorably put it, "Beer just goes with pizza."

I love that Mom loves all these little nuisances about her, but I'm surprised she wants to include the part about Sadie sipping a small shot of Scotch out of a little skinny shot glass each morning in her latter years (sometime after breakfast, but never before her daily prayers). I was hesitant to include this part of her life story, thinking it would give you the wrong idea, but as it turns out, it was just Sadie—being Sadie—a naturalist born before her time!

PART IV

Jean, Tina, Mary, and our mom

CHAPTER 10

On Being a Mother

Despite being a busy mother of six girls, with plenty of cotton outfits to iron, cleaning and laundry to do, plus lunches to make, I can always find time for a cup of tea with Sadie. I try to emulate her, by caring for and loving my girls the way she cares for her children, especially seeing how they love and respect her in return. Sadie admits raising children is a learning experience for all parents, and my wanting her to come for a visit is particularly true when I'm overwhelmed and need to be reminded of my mommy commitment. I invite her today.

I fill her fancy china cup to the brim with boiling hot water for the Sanka, just the way she likes it. She sits down at my little kitchen table and I'm in my glory as I pour myself a cup of tea and gently lean back in my chair while she delicately sips the instant black coffee from her teacup, gingerly holding it with a lightly-polished pinky finger gently extended. "Today's lesson is— 'On Being a Mother' and much like the five fingers on your hands are each different, so too each of your children will be different, and should be treated as such."

Most mothers can attest to this fact, whether they have two children or eight (like her). Sadie's wisdom certainly rings true for me. My six girls are like night and day and seriously everything in between. Susan is jovial. Marie is deep and my Tina resembles my Jimmie in so many ways you could easily mistake his childhood photo for hers. Jeanne, the other middle child, is shy and quiet, and the only authentic-looking Sicilian is Toni Ann with reddish-golden curly hair, she's my father all over again and has a bit of Jimmie thrown in with his outgoing and delightfully social personality.

Anne Marie will always be the baby of the family and has many of Sadie's insightful and warm-hearted tendencies. Yet regardless of children's many differences, getting a message across to a teenager is a challenge; ask any parent, teacher, or guardian. Sadie calls this tough message, "The Hole in the Mountain."

Teenagers are inclined to tune-out authority figures, and oftentimes you start to think you sound like a broken record when repeating important reminders, no child should ignore. "Never talk to strangers," and "Don't walk down the alley alone at night," are serious ones. I had all girls, mind you, so these are the ones that readily come to mind, not to mention the multitude of mundane, but rather important reminders like, "Please finish your homework before dinner," and the easily recognizable, "Don't forget to your brush teeth." It's a seemingly thankless job and seems as if what you're saying isn't sinking in to anyone's head, except yours.

Sadie wants to lighten up the mood by depositing this gem of a message that has become my new favorite analogy. "Much like water continually dripping on a mountain in one spot will eventually leave a hole for the water to get through (and possibly the sunshine), so too your consistency will make a lasting impression on the children."

My daughters, Susan and Marie are teenagers and cute Tina isn't far behind, so I can easily relate to this message these days. I've made some mistakes along the way trying to teach my daughters right from wrong, and may have reprimanded one child more than others or possibly favored the easy ones, but sometimes personality clashes can make it more difficult to be the best parent you can be. This could also be the reason parenting techniques change for every child despite your best efforts to treat them all fairly, and may be why every parent-child relationship is completely different. But instead of feeling guilty for my past mistakes, I accept them, and do what I can to improve myself and the relationships with my daughters.

Remember, if you're consistent with the methods, they'll eventually get the picture and the reminders will pay off for you and your children. That's what Sadie teaches and reminds me of whenever I am doubtful. She continually displays a tremendous ability to mother with gentle, firm truths. That is her gift, which she gives freely to anyone willing to embrace it. I find myself listening intently as Sadie continues: "As God the Father is head of the church, so too the father of your children is the head of the home and should be honored as such."

⸺◡ **Tina and her beautiful daughters . . .** ◠⸺
Susan, Marie, Tina, Jeanne, Toni Ann and Anne Marie

There are parents who may, knowingly or unknowingly, pit their spouses against the children, or put the children and their needs and desires first. When this happens, and it can happen a lot, the happiness of the home can be at stake and may cause everyone in the family unnecessary grief.

Sadie has the answer.

"To be a good mother, you must first be a committed wife, having both love and respect for your husband. In order to do this right, your priority is to make the home a comfortable place for your spouse, while providing a safe, loving environment for the children." That is the correct order of things, yet many do not want to admit it.

Not so with Sadie's daughter Jeanne, who's happily married with three children of her own and confidently displays a plaque with a similar sentiment about commitment. The proof isn't in the plaque hanging on the wall, it's in the way Jeanne demonstrates her undying love for Mike, who genuinely adores her in a way far deeper than any poetic words. An unselfish willingness to honor and cherish her husband in that same way was the greatest gift Sadie gave to us girls. She closes with this admirable quote, "The greatest gift any mother can give to her children is to truly love their father."

Sadie cannot say it any clearer.

CHAPTER 11

Blessings in Disguise

It's a typical winter day and my little one is about to turn three. The unforeseen happens, and I ask myself, "Why us?"

I'm feeling guilty for even thinking it, but Jimmie and I are living through one of life's tougher times. I notice Marie is getting a little chunky, but since fluctuations in weight are common for teenage girls, I think nothing of it, until Marie starts complaining about not feeling well. She wants to stay home from school again today, so I decide to take her to the local doctor to get some answers, but he can't find anything wrong with her. I'm really worried.

With Carmela by my side for support, we bring Marie to our favorite doctor (from the old neighborhood) for a second opinion. He examines Marie, then calls us into his office and says carefully, "You might have been thinking Marie is sick, but she's okay." That's a big relief until he says a second later, "Marie is seven-and-a-half months pregnant."

This news nearly causes me to faint.

I never suspected this would happen to us and certainly not to Marie. After all, she and Jimmie have the best rapport, she's the son he never had; a strong, dependable, and capable girl. As a matter of fact, a few hours earlier, Marie stood up on a ladder to help Jimmie hang the famous wall-to-wall mural of an Italian villa which appears in the background of countless numbers of family photos. It was eight-year-old Marie again, in the Blizzard of '58 (after 30 inches of snow had fallen) who helped Jimmie put chains on the tires the night I gave birth to our fourth child.

You're probably thinking I'm a parent who doesn't have a clue what's going on with my child. I've been there, judging others who've dealt with similar situations, but believe me—finding yourself in the dark where your child is concerned can happen to anyone. I considered Marie might be pregnant several months ago, yet I promptly dismissed it, reasoning Marie isn't dating anyone. Besides, with six girls, ages three to eighteen still living at home, it's almost impossible to imagine. But nonetheless, in less than two months, I will be a grandmother.

The doctor suggests we tell our family that Marie had a nervous breakdown, or I could go away with her and act as if the baby is mine. I'm not sure what to do, so I take a walk to the church to clear my head and to talk with our parish priest. While waiting in the front pew, I'm feeling a strong sense of relief, thinking the priest will have a godly perspective and offer thought-felt answers to my many questions.

The opposite happens.

The priest immediately begins speaking of a nice Catholic couple wanting to adopt and strongly suggests Marie consider giving up her baby. He lists the potential downsides of keeping the child including the negative impact on the other girls, and how difficult this would be with three little ones of my own. This option was a common solution for unwed mothers in those days, so I don't slight the priest or the doctor for their advice or for mentioning we visit the Home of the Guardian Angels, a place many girls stay waiting to give birth; where most will have to put their babies up for adoption. There is no choice for these young girls, I understand this, but I can't imagine letting this happen to my daughter.

That's all well and good, since as soon as we exit the home Marie tell me she's not going to consider it. Only a few months ago we were celebrating Marie's sweet sixteenth birthday, and now she's going to be a mother. As we're walking toward the bus stop, Marie offers to tell her father about the baby and doesn't seem the slightest bit worried about it.

Boy, are we different.

Or maybe it's that I think I know my husband better than she knows her father. Jimmie reacts rather calmly to her news, and its Jimmie who bravely decides to call Sadie to bring all his brothers and sisters together for a family gathering where he'll tell them Marie is pregnant, and about her decision to keep the baby. He says he doesn't want rumors to start flying around the neighborhood if he can help it, and puts his faith in what Sadie likes to call, "Respecting the Horse for the Master." Jimmie explains precisely what's happening in our household, and politely asks them to show their support and respect. Jimmie is the father (master of the home) and everyone should respect his daughter and future grandchild because of it.

They all agree, but that's not the end of our worries.

While changing his diaper only a few months after he's born, Susan's friend's mom asks in the most innocent way, "I didn't realize you had a son, Tina." She's seems embarrassed when I explain James Anthony is Marie's son; but I assure her that my youngest is four years old and Toni Ann is only in first grade, so it could make sense. In all, there are nine people living in our house and we're dealing with these changes differently. Just when our lives seem to be getting back to normal, James Anthony starts to call me mommy. I realize we can't keep raising our grandson as if he is our son. We adore him in every way imaginable, but he's Marie's son, so we sit down with her and explain it is probably best she be a full-time mom to James Anthony. This means more change, perhaps too much, but it's the best choice.

Relief comes with trips to Sadie's house.

I need her wisdom and to be around her calming ways. I find myself at her house more frequently than usual. Sometimes she joins me in a good cry, however I didn't realize my problems were affecting my dear friend, apparently leaving her upset after my visits. Sadie's youngest son, Anthony, asks Carmela to please ask me to limit my visits, so I do. He has Sadie's best interest at heart, and is completely right, but no matter how much I want to, I can't seem to make peace with what is happening in our lives.

No one seems to question when you go to a medical doctor if you have pains in your chest or a cold you can't get rid of, but what happens if you want to go to a doctor who treats the mind? Sadie encourages me not to worry about that. My decision to see a therapist ultimately comes down to her tender advice, "Tina, if you believe therapy will help you, by all means give it a try. Even if people in the neighborhood talk or say you're crazy, you know that it's not true." I'm nervous before the first session, but the look of our psychologist, a younger version of Burl Ives, is comforting as I enter the room full of strangers. With Sadie's extra boost of confidence, I start the weekly sessions and attend the group on a regular basis. I'm given the tools I need to overcome the obstacles in my way. Afterwards, I'm led to Melvin Katz for one-on-one private sessions, and this man becomes my very own Dr. Phil. He makes me face my life. I thank God every day for those life truths and for him, wherever he might be.

At this moment, here's how I define my life. I'm sweet Tina, a thirty-nine-year-old grandmother with little ones of my own, working the lunch crowd from behind the counter at Josie's Deli, glad it's only around the corner from our house and I'm making the best of it.

And just as Sadie said, "Everything is going to be all right."

My turnaround is dependent on many other saving graces, and though some of the troubles we experienced were exactly what the priest said might happen, none of us have regret when it comes to having James Anthony in our lives. This little boy has made our family stronger. In the end, life is about making the choice to accept change, and by making this personal choice, you will be happier and a better person for it.

I know I am.

And James Anthony is absolutely living proof the best things in life are truly the blessings in disguise.

Sadie, Marie, James Anthony
Mary and Jimmie – 1969

On Being Family

BY ANNE MARIE

Mom comes up with some pretty funny lines, however at times her comments can come across on the harsh side. This worries me, I'm afraid people will take her the wrong way and that would be a real shame, since she's a genuinely warm and kind person, and everyone loves her dearly. So I soften her commentary.

Recollections of summer nights spent at the bungalow in West Oak Recreation Club are sharp for Mom, including a wonderful story about Sadie visiting when she was well into her seventies. This time we're teaching, and Sadie is learning, learning how to play the game of Pit. It starts with a bell, and in this case, eight loud Italians trying to buy, sell, and trade our cards of wheat, barley, oats, and other grains.

Tina's face lights up as she reminisces.

I remember this muggy night on Long Island. Sadie is seated in the middle of our sticky mustard-yellow leather circular booth while we rouse the quiet country night and the neighbors by slamming the bell; yelling flax, wheat, or possibly oats, and quickly throwing down our cards to make the fastest trades—and lasting memories.

Not only did we have a bungalow, so did Sadie's daughters Carmela, Jeanne and Marie, who was the one who first bought a bungalow after the local pool was shut down, and now our families had a new place to go for the summers. The West Oak Recreation Club had more Italians than they probably wanted

⟋⌒ New Year's Day at Capriccio's ~ 2005 ⌒⟍
Jimmie and his sisters, Jeanne and Carmela

and they never saw this clan coming. My Aunt Marie and Aunt Carmela each had a bungalow near the Marina; our family lived near the creek and the "crooked-mile" that led to the coves with the best fishing, and crabbing, for those delicious blue-claw crabs. And last, but not least, Aunt Jeanne lived on the other end of the community, much closer to the beach. Our families loved it!

For the first few years we worked on the book, Mom and I called on Aunt Jeanne often. She told us terrific stories about the nuisances of my Grandma Sadie. To give us a delightfully different perspective, we call on my Aunt Carmela, who is dear to Tina's heart, as is her sister, Jeanne, whose gorgeous smile and distinctively raspy laugh lights up any room she enters. Luckily, Aunt Carmela knew all the right answers to my difficult questions regarding Sadie's lessons. To Tina, these women were kindred spirits from the moment they met, and these lifelong friendships mean so much to her, solidly-based in mutual respect and a family love that has never wavered.

Hearing these stories first-hand, plus the extraordinarily nice things people say about my mom convinces me (despite her admitted mistakes) that she did a terrific job raising us girls, and her point of view is far more valid than I originally thought. Not to mention the unmistakable love all these women have for their husbands, children, and grandchildren; and the unmistakable love and adoration they receive in return.

Wow, they're all like Sadie.

Mom can no longer hide her enthusiasm and confides in Angela about the book, who is genuinely thrilled with the idea. According to Mom, it wasn't a coincidence that on a hot summer day when my dad was working at the Sports Center Bowl and he hears a voice he's sure he knows. "Hey, that's my cousin Angela," he says to a co-worker as he turns to get her attention. Smiles fly across the bowling alley when Angela sees my dad, Jimmie, and family is reunited—thousands of miles away from Brooklyn.

Angela's budding family invites all of us to their home for many family gatherings, especially if her Aunt Sadie is in town. This chance encounter forges a lasting friendship between our families, and means at least ten extra guests at Angela's whenever Sadie visits. Sadie was around sixty-years-old and a grandmother to many when her niece asks if she will be the godmother to her baby daughter. After a bit of reluctance, worrying about her age, Sadie accepts this special honor. Tina loves the story and asks Angela if she would like to write something in honor of her Aunt Sadie.

Here's a portion of Angela's heartfelt, eerily apropos letter:

It was an honor to have Aunt Sadie as my godmother, if only to prove how much she meant to my mother. Early memories as a very young child were of special visits to what to me felt like a foreign, faraway place—Brooklyn. We were always exuberantly greeted at the door by the beautifully dressed from head-to-toe Sadie, and a house full of relatives, friends, food, and laughter. Aunt Sadie may have been in her seventies and eighties when I knew her best, but she was always young at heart! And at my daughter, Grace Mary's baptism, Sadie was ninety-four, still perky and perfectly dressed, with a warm touch, beautiful smile, and wishes of good luck, good health, and happiness always!

~ Angela

As it turns out, Angela is a terrific wife and mother in her own right, and her words are a perfect fit for Sadie. When my cousin Angela and her husband, Jim, invite us to witness the baptism of their baby daughter, I am lucky enough to sit in the front pew right alongside my Grandma Sadie. It was amazing to be present for such a significant and joyous event, as was hearing Angela's sincere encouragement to my mom to finish writing *Sadie's Pearls*, no matter how long it takes us.

PART V

~∽ **Tina relishing a night out on the town** ∾~
Lake Tahoe, CA ~ 1978

CHAPTER 12

On Being a Grandmother

It's winter—if you can call any day in Los Angeles winter.

I'm on my way to visit Jimmie at Henry Mayo, for what feels like day one-thousand-and-one of coming to this place. Yet something about this hospital stay seems different from the rest, despite having been under these similar circumstances many times before. I guess eight hours a day in one spot for this many months in a row makes it feel that way.

Jimmie yearns for my presence daily. He wants me at the hospital no later than noon, every day; otherwise he thinks I'm out having fun while he's all cooped up. Jimmie's aged a bit (diabetes surely has taken its toll), but luckily his ever-bright smile, charm, and true love remain reminding me of how blessed I am, every day, even on days like today, when his temper flares upon my grand entrance.

I had hoped a family visit would've occupied Jimmie and kept his mind off the clock—but it didn't.

Jimmie's aware my son-in-law is my stand-in, and regardless of this opportunity to spend time with our grandson

Stephen, none of it will make up for the fact that I am running really late. At three-and-a-half years old and after being here for over two hours, Stephen starts acting a bit rambunctious, running up and down the hallways, and then climbing on and off the bed. Jimmie is getting agitated, and this is clearly not the place for such gymnastics, so I gently remind him, "Stephen, please sit down and relax for a while, and no more running and jumping in here, you might get hurt."

To my comment his father responds, "Oh Ma, you're such a neurotic." I knew it was coming as the words, "you might get hurt" spilled out of my mouth. I admit I'm on the overly cautious side, since accidents are still one of the leading causes of death in children. I'm well aware children need time to play and explore, but it isn't neurotic to be preventive or to force downtime, especially in the cramped space of a hospital room. I want to say more in my defense, and in defense of children everywhere, but I realize this is neither the time, nor the place.

I would love to be sitting here reminiscing with Jimmie about the good old days living in Brooklyn; meeting and falling in love, raising our six daughters, and the most unexpected good times in the late 1970s when Jimmie and I and our three youngest girls move to California.

But that's just not us.

Susan was working as an executive at Casablanca Records in Hollywood before our move to Sherman Oaks. We live south of the boulevard in a modern ranch-style home with a secluded yard which encircles the house (a far cry from our fenced-in cramped backyard back in Brooklyn). We're reaping in the benefits of living like movie stars, and you might guess it from a widely-popular family photo of Susan perched upon a pristine blue mailbox at the corner of Farragut Road and 42nd Street (steps away from our Calder house). Susan is looking highly sophisticated; slender legs dangling perfectly from underneath her fancy dress, like this is a scene from a Hollywood movie, and the sparkling city belongs to her. I should've suspected the fun times we'd have meeting superstars in the decades following our big move to California. Many of our favorite photos lined our hallway walls for decades; me, the superstars, and Jimmie (with his ever-beaming smile) posing for the iconic photos while savoring in these special moments of our life.

But that was then, and this is now.

Jimmie retires again in the 1980s (this time from the bowling alley) and we move thirty miles north to the growing town of Saugus. We're enjoying a much quieter lifestyle, spending most of our days enjoying our fabulous corner backyard. Jimmie is tending to his raised vegetable garden or barbequing steaks while I whip up peppers and onions in the kitchen. I happily peer through my corner window with a full view of Jimmie, the pool, and his gorgeous roses circling the background.

This is really the life.

⌒ **With matching smiles** ⌒

Jimmie and his mom, Sadie
Sherman Oaks, CA

⌒ **Living the good life ~ Tina and Sadie** ⌒

Bel Air, CA

During the summer, my daughter Jeanne and her two kids visit from Castaic at least three times a week, and Toni Ann and my grandson Stephen live a mile away, so they're here almost every day, especially when their big sister Tina visits with her three kids to see us, but mainly to get away from their cramped apartment and the typical ninety-percent humidity of Brooklyn.

As I'm watching from the window, Christi Anne is swimming exuberantly in the pool while her brothers, Anthony and James, play joyfully in the unheated swirling Jacuzzi. These happy thoughts fill my heart with joy for the moment, and remind me of the memorable times spent at Saturday morning picnics when all of our families lived in Brooklyn. Most of the husbands went to the park early to secure every picnic table, and they were cooking breakfast by the time we arrived with too many kids to count. Sunday gatherings at Sadie's brought a new set of challenges; the house obviously didn't have the accommodations of a park, and there were more and more mouths to feed, so we ate in shifts. First, the dads and husbands were served at the dining room table, then the children, and finally the woman ate in relative peace while the men kept an eye on the little ones. The cycle repeated itself when the coffee and cake were served as the little ones anxiously awaited their turn for dessert on the bustling outdoor patio.

However, I still find myself a bit irked by Stephen's father's earlier comment, "Oh Ma, you're such a neurotic." Sadie's words enter my mind; they are strong, clear, and seem to come from deep within. "Better they should cry, than you cry."

Why does one always think of the perfect thing to say after the moment has gone?

I'm tempted to repeat the phrase out loud, right to him, but I hold my tongue and even smile a little on the inside; knowing exactly what I'll do instead. Jimmie and I have been happily married for over forty-eight years and have been sweethearts for as long as I can remember, so there is no other place I'd rather be.

It's just that I never expected to spend our precious retirement moments watching days, weeks, and what seem like years, ticking away inside this many drab hospital rooms. So after they bid their goodbyes, I take out a pen, my spiral notebook, and as Jimmie comfortably rests in his hospital bed, happily occupied with *Judge Judy*—I begin to write.

Our Precious Grandchildren

James Anthony, Neil, Vincent, and Michael ~ 1980s

Christi Anne, Anthony, John Michael,
James, Christine, and Stephen - 1990s

CHAPTER 13

Better They Should Cry

Stephen is my tenth and youngest grandchild.

Over the years for the sake of my daughters' children, I've done quite a bit of childproofing in my house; it's dramatically different from what I did while raising them. Don't get me wrong, my grandchildren aren't more rambunctious than my daughters were at their ages (however I'm equally aware of the dangers found inside the home) so when my little ones weren't able to be supervised properly, they were generally confined to a highchair, playpen or carriage.

If you have ever tried the popular candy Life Savers, you may have wondered why it has a hole in the middle, but the famous hole isn't just a marketing gimmick.

It's there for safety reasons.

In case you swallow the candy whole and it gets stuck, you would still be able to breathe. With this reasoning behind the design of the candy, wouldn't you agree that safety is a good idea, perhaps the best idea? I believe children sometimes need to be confined to a playpen or a highchair, especially toddlers, anytime you cannot give them your full attention. To that end, Sadie would gleefully report, "If you know the baby is fed, changed, and not sick, it's okay to lay them down in the crib."

"They may cry. Babies cry."

"Better they should cry than you cry," may not be a popular message any more today than it was in my day, but it's one I continue to advocate, keeping in mind that statistically more children under the age of four die from accidents than from all childhood diseases combined, so it never hurts to be proactive.

A child may cry if you put him in a playpen or take away a dangerous toy, but sometimes you need to make the choice. There were many times my girls would feign crying or complain incessantly about how their lives would be ruined if I didn't let them do what they wanted to do. I was frustrated; teenagers are frustrating, but I remain steadfast, and put my rules first.

Sadie would sum up her lesson on how to raise kids this way, "It's a lot easier to say yes, but saying no is the real gift."

I heard one of the saddest stories of my life many decades ago, but I will never forget it. A mother explains how she left her ten-month-old child unattended on the living room floor, for a moment, to answer the ringing phone. Seems harmless enough, but when she returns, her son has pulled a crystal ashtray onto his head. He was permanently brain damaged from the accident, leaving her to wish she could turn back the hands of time for one minute. She can't.

I was crying when she ends by saying that she has to live with this the rest of her life, and so does her son. Their lives changed forever. However, I'm fully aware accidents can happen in an instant and they can't always be prevented, but there's nothing wrong with being cautious, or perhaps a bit more neurotic. After all, safety is important.

I was pretty annoyed the day when my son-in-law said I was a neurotic. But I truly thank him because it reminded me of Sadie's saying, "Better they should cry than you cry," and it is exactly what motivated me to begin writing these stories.

Yet nothing is as important as the chance it has given me—to give you—a rare glimpse into the life of Sadie.

CHAPTER 14

I Can Take Children All Day

What I truly cannot understand is why the average child, including my own grandchildren, stay up so late—half of them nowadays into the middle of the night.

No one seems to be setting rules and regulations for their children, often depriving parents of the quiet time needed to relax, talk amongst adults, or handle important tasks without interruption. Kids today are obsessed with phones, computers, and video games which makes it more difficult for parents to set bedtimes that are early enough, even though twenty-first century doctors still recommend children get about ten hours of sleep a night. The demands of modern life make this a major challenge.

Children's lives today are filled with too much home-work, excessive extra-curricular activities, and countless gadgets. There doesn't seem to be enough quality time left for family, and a fast-paced lifestyle can rob children of the joys of simply being children. Chaos has a way of growing out of disorganization, so I decide early on that it will be my job to organize my girls and teach them light cleaning and some other chores. I want them to know the basics when it comes to taking care of themselves, but not without losing sight of their place as children or as teenagers.

There is time enough for them to be adults later.

My sisters and I had plenty of fun growing up. We were always playing games, inside and outside, with each other and with friends, but we knew our limits (beds were made before school, toys were put away when we were done playing, and clothes were never strewn about our rooms in utter chaos). We knew exactly what could and couldn't be done in the Guzzo household—and we listened to our mother—most of the time.

After my girls return from school, they change out of their school uniforms and into play clothes. But before going outside, they confirm their homework is done. Before dinner, I make sure they put away toys, clothes and any school books lying around the house while I prepare the evening meal. Following dinner, they clear the dishes and then get ready for bed. They are in their rooms at eight o'clock on weeknights. Sometimes I hear them laughing and talking, long after I say lights out, but when I yell up the stairs, "Don't let me come up there," the noise dies down to nothing but soft giggles.

The fact is, once you start having kids, you have to set specific rules and regulations, otherwise you will never find enough time to get important things done or get a little peace and quiet. Although no one has heard Sadie utter the words, "I can take children all day, but not all night," I believe she practiced it and I would like to believe she agrees with its message, no matter how quirky.

Tonight, what's most important to me is that my girls are where they're supposed to be, when they're supposed to be there. However, some parents may let their children influence important family decisions or in other words, let the children rule-the-roost. This could be due to several factors in our modern society including the prevalence of two working parents, divorce, and the not so simple, blending of families. I can understand changes happen in life, but you must be careful to recognize that when you find new love, things may not work out quite so well for your children.

As a parent you must be careful not to blame children for the normal difficulties which occur in every new relationship, especially when they themselves may be having a difficult time with the big changes in their lives. Plenty of well-meaning people (including happily married couples) find themselves in a variety of tough situations and may make a habit overindulging them as a way of compensating, thinking they can buy their children's acceptance with gifts, but gifts can never replace you.

Jimmie and I tried our best to provide balance and guidance, and formed a united front when dealing with issues concerning our girls, and that is all I can ask anyone to do. We weren't perfect, and they didn't always listen to our good advice or make the best choices for their lives, but if you raise children with proper boundaries, teach them respect, show them love, and treat them with the dignity they deserve, you'll be giving them a real chance at a successful life. And if they depart someday from the path you set before them, there will always be the possibility of their return to a good path for their lives, and to the family. At least that's what you hope, yet children sometimes need to learn life lessons their own way, and for some, in the hardest way.

It's interesting how many children mimic and aspire to be like their parents when they are kids, fight not to be like them when they are teenagers, and think they have completely succeeded by their twenties, only to find out, lo and behold, by age thirty they are more like their parents than they ever thought possible. Later on in life, we may even be willing to admit our true blessings are wrapped up in the crazy things of family that we've been trying to avoid all along.

The phrase, "The fruit doesn't fall far from the tree," is one I believe is a truth, but Anne Marie wonders about the children who don't fall so close to the family tree, or the ones who leave and never come back. Anne Marie puts it this way. "The fruit doesn't fall far from the tree, or it rolls very, very, far away."

So be it.

Another quirky idiom the family uses at the exact moment a person makes a profound statement as the proverbial dish drops, or door slams, is a resounding, "It's

True!" It is said swiftly, loudly, and in perfect unison, as if the harmonious nature adds credence to the truth spoken.

I use the phrase all the time, we all do, and so does Sadie.

One afternoon I mention to Sadie that my girls are fighting over chores and I don't want to be the one to punish them later, but they're going to need to be grounded. I'm overwhelmed.

She softly replies, "Don't worry, Tina, they're just kids being kids, and their behavior is perfectly normal; but you really must put your foot down, Tina. It's really not a good idea to always leave the reprimanding for Jimmie, making him out to be the bad guy. And, never forget your children didn't ask to be brought into the world." I came to understand the deeper meaning of this crucial statement for parents, and its obligation that is without compromise.

I came to this conclusion with Sadie's help.

My girls were arguing over who should wash the dishes and who should take care of the other chores I gave them to do today, as if they're in a position to make the call, but here we are. When I discuss the situation with Jimmie after dinner, that very night he takes the time to make a complete list with their names, the days of the week, and each household chore that needs to be completed. He even goes as far as assigning a specific length of time to complete each task, so there'll be no dallying. This puts an end to that argument, because once it's written down by their father, it is law.

I'm back in charge and peace is restored.

Peace comes when you create boundaries for children of any given age, and a clear indication certain things are expected of them is a necessary part of parenting. I needed a reminder. Good results may not happen the first, second, or tenth time you instruct your children, but they will happen. My oldest daughter Susan does her best to overcome Jimmie's new chore list for the foreseeable future, by taking the money she earns (and saves) from a part-time job to buy us a dishwasher as our twentieth anniversary present.

"What a gift and what an absolutely wonderful daughter," I say as I'm loading the brand new dishwasher. The rest of our girls are not so easily convinced, they know the gift was a convenient way for her to get out of washing dishes for the foreseeable future, and it's probably true, since Susan's not-so-endearing, but long-lasting family nickname is, "The Queen."

And true to form, Queens, and now Susan, don't do dishes.

Who's the Mother?

ANNE MARIE

"Who's the Mother?" had been our working title from the beginning of this journey, until the day my mom is at Stanley's Restaurant on Ventura Boulevard for lunch with Susan, and renowned singer and family friend, Donna Summer. She tells her, "I'm absolutely convinced your book should be called *Sadie's Pearls*, Tina."

As predicted, Mom is out and about more than she's at the house working, but she's so excited about the news she calls me from the restaurant. I'm honestly shocked, and do my best to convince my mom to keep the original title with many valid reasons and the most important reason of all, "It's been our working title for over three years."

They fall on deaf ears. So "Sadie's Pearls" it is.

The moment I finally give in, it's like a giant light bulb goes off in my head, so I say to Mom, "That's why I can't imagine Grandma Sadie saying, 'I can take children all day, but not all night!'" Mom confesses that this saying, along with the original title belong to her, and by the end of the day, we discover several other lessons are hers too. She's disappointed after we decide those lessons need to be cut, even though she agrees the book is meant to be a tribute to Sadie's pearls of wisdom, and not hers, after all. To her growing sadness, I sweetly add, "Don't worry, Mom, you can always put those lessons in your next book." We start laughing pretty hard, not because it's funny to think of an eighty-five-year-old starting to write another book when her first one isn't even finished, but because the original working title, "Who's the Mother?" fits her perfectly.

So much enlightenment over a cup of tea!

By taking everything my mom learned from Sadie and her mother, plus the things we have since learned together has been nothing short of a miracle. I'm pretty lucky to be the baby of her large close-knit family (the kind she always wanted), born on St. Patrick's Day only a mere eight days after the golden charm bracelet was given to my future Grandma Sadie.

Despite Mom's repeated pleas to Dad to name me Patricia, I wasn't. Luckily, since I don't have the fair skin or reddish hair to go with the festive Irish holiday on which I was born. On the contrary, I look Italian, with olive skin, soft brown eyes and lots of dark wavy hair, and the name Anne Marie fits me perfectly.

Anne Marie's
⌒ **First Communion** ⌒

On the porch at our
Brooklyn home

—⟨⟩ **Our Beautiful Daughters** ⟨⟩—
Susan, Jeanne, Toni Ann, Marie, Tina, and Anne Marie

As with all the momentous times of your life, holidays spent with friends and family are the real highlight of life, and the years spent with Donna and her family were delightful, with lots of family love, crazy fun, and without a doubt, delicious food.

Donna and her family were major fans of my Grandma Sadie's recipe, "Spaghetti and Nuts." A unique, signature Serpico dish reserved for Christmas Eve dinners. Many times their equally rambunctious and loving family spent several holidays with us, chopping and chopping various nuts, followed by everyone enjoying a fancy feast at Susan's house in Bel Air.

**Sadie and
Donna Summer having
a blast**

Atlantic City,
New Jersey ~ 1980s

Donna adores Sadie's ever youthful spirit and admires her willingness to go with the flow on any given holiday or spur of the moment hotel adventure. Sadie was fast approaching her seventy-ninth birthday when she stayed up well into the night with Susan after Donna's performance. She is thoroughly enjoying a little gambling at an old-fashioned slot machine, the kind where you put the coins in manually and pull a lever to make it work. Susan is too tired to stay up and says, "Come on; let's head up to the suite."

Sadie looks up and replies, "I'll be up later; I'm winning."

Early the next morning, Susan wakes up wondering, "Where is Grandma Sadie? She hasn't even slept in her bed."

In a panic, Susan rushes downstairs to find Sadie sitting in the same chair, at the same slot machine, oblivious to the time. She casually looks up, with black fingers and buckets full of nickels sitting nearby, she smiles brightly. Susan can tell she's pretty ecstatic. Relief and wonder diminish her worries, and when they cash it in, Susan laughs—it's barely eighty dollars.

Every person who had the opportunity to meet Sadie was blessed by her presence in a personal way. She was always there when you needed her to be there, with words of wisdom or just her warm presence. And while "Who's the Mother?" may not be the title of this book or any other book, choosing *Sadie's Pearls* as our title is not only a loving tribute to Donna Summer, it accomplishes Mom's true purpose—to honor Sadie.

PART VI

~ Beautiful Sadie posing in Hollywood ~

Florida - 1980s

CHAPTER 15

Lasting Gifts

Sadie moves to Hollywood, Florida, like many retired New Yorkers, to get away from the cold winters and to help relieve her increasing arthritis. My Susan's career takes her to Hollywood, California.

A few years later Jimmie and I make the move to the West Coast. We purchase a nice home in the hills of Sherman Oaks. It's a four bedroom which is perfect with our three youngest daughters still living at home. Unfortunately, we're three-thousand miles away from Sadie now, but regardless of where I am living, I make it a point to visit her as often as I can.

Sadie was around eighty-years-old when her daughter, Jeanne, has a friend's wedding to attend and asks her if she can borrow the gold-braided necklace and matching earrings that were a gift from the children on her sixtieth birthday. She doesn't hesitate in saying yes, and to Jeanne's surprise, when she tries to return the necklace and the earrings, Sadie expresses what's in her heart, "Since you love this jewelry so much, I would love for you to keep them."

I believe this was the first day Sadie began giving away more than treasured jewels of wisdom. Sadie is well aware of what can happen when children are left to distribute the belongings of a deceased parent, and knows first-hand the unnecessary grief and family upheaval it can bring with it. So she decides early on to save her children from this fate by taking many pieces of her jewelry collection and giving them away, in a warm gesture, genuinely touching their hearts, and leaving lasting memories.

This is what she gives—but she doesn't stop there.

Over the next twenty years, Sadie gives her children most of their inheritance, in generous increments, quietly and sweetly—but with tremendous joy, like the way her children gave beautiful corsages on Mother's Day—as if to say, "I love you!" Even for a woman as financially savvy as her, this is a huge feat for a widow on a fixed income, yet Sadie accomplishes it.

In the 1990s, Jimmie and I live in La Grangeville, New York, (a country town about two hours from Manhattan) in a fabulous high-ranch style home with a larger vegetable garden for Jimmie to tend to. We're like Sadie, wanting to be near at least one of our children, so accordingly, our home on Charlotte Drive is less than a mile from our daughter Jeanne.

On a warm afternoon in May, I'm out with my Jeanne shopping at the Danbury Mall, because Jeanne loves the mall, and I love getting out of the house when the weather is nice. I'm strolling around the mall when I see a plaque hanging in one of the novelty gift shops and it makes me laugh; the words remind me of something Sadie used to say, "It's not living if you're worrying about everything in your life being perfect."

Let me explain a bit further. Jeanne's husband, John, is a doll of a person, and a one-in-a-million son-in-law, but he can be somewhat overly concerned when it comes to added expenses in the budget. He shouldn't be, he's also one of the best savers I know. Though I'm not sure Jeanne is going to get the same kick out of the plaque as I did, she laughs when I take her to see it.

I tell her I am thinking of buying it to lift his spirits after an unforeseen expense came his way last week, but mainly because it isn't often we get to this awesome mall in Connecticut.

The plaque reads:

Just When You Think the Ends Will Meet, Somebody Moves the Ends.

That's right, things happen in life, even when you think you have the perfect plan in place, things don't work out your way. There are countless opportunities to learn from this lesson and it meshes remarkably well with Sadie's adage telling us to choose a happy life because unexpected things will happen all the time. John may have good reason to worry, so I thought he deserved something special: a hug, a soft word from Sadie, or this fun plaque?

I could remind John, this should be the worst that ever happens, but that wouldn't be nice. This gift is a much better way to express my feelings." When I get home, I remind John that everything will work out and he can easily handle the expense with his organized budget. Sadie is not here to offer more profound advice, and no hugs were exchanged between us, but John appreciates the thoughtful gesture and the pleasant reminder, besides, even sweet Sadie was known to take frugality to a whole new level.

My daughter Tina can distinctly remember standing near Sadie's kitchen entry to help serve dessert at her grandmother's house and hearing Sadie say to the adults, "The kids don't need a whole plate for this small piece of cake," as she proceeded to cut the paper plates in half. Then she instructs my Tina to cut the napkins while quietly asking, "Oh, why should we let them waste a whole napkin when a half a napkin will be just as good?" Sadie had a tendency to cut paper towels in half decades before it was sold in stores; another one of her savvy ideas— eventually adopted by an entire industry.

Sadie's lasting gifts were hearing the stories, learning the lessons, and receiving the treasured memories; gifts to anyone willing to listen. And many did. Sadie gives traditions a wider lens from which to see and makes them captivating as if she knows they're the true spice of life. Traditions give us something to look forward to, every year, especially when you spice up the holidays

~⟨ **Mary, Santa, and Sadie** ⟩~
Hollywood, FL

~⟨ **Sadie, Santa, and Jimmie** ⟩~
Hollywood, CA

with pickled herring or a parade of carnation pomp and circumstance.

In one of the priceless photos we recently located, my mom is resting on the corner of Santa's left leg, while Sadie rests comfortably on his other knee, presumably to tell him what they want for Christmas. They're laughing and smiling together, and having a real blast. Just like Sadie and me.

Always remember, when Sadie tells you, "Life is easier if you enjoy it," she's depositing a treasure, hoping you'll do your best to follow her advice by getting as much happiness as you possibly can out of your life.

Everyone should be like Sadie—who gave away her greatest treasures—while her eyes were still open.

**Sadie looking
as stylish as ever . . .**

. . . wearing her treasured
gold necklace

CHAPTER 16

Sadie's Ninetieth Birthday

It's an ordinary summer night in 1988 in Oakdale, Long Island, when my sister-in-law Jeanne, her husband Mike, and their son Gregory decide to plan a surprise ninetieth birthday party for Sadie.

Much like a wedding, it would take a year of planning to pull off the big surprise. They had to pick the perfect venue, send the fancy invitations, buy arrangements with Sadie's favorite flowers, carefully choose the menu (to please everyone), hire the band, and create a detailed seating chart (again, to please everyone). To represent all of Sadie's birthdays, Jeanne has to purchase five boxes of candles to be sure they have ninety candles, plus one, for good luck. Who could've imagined they'd be able to get every last gleaming candle on the cake? When Jeanne summons the family to tell them about the big surprise party they are planning for Sadie, everyone gladly offers to chip in to be sure this milestone happens in a grand way.

Sadie's birthday lands in the middle of the week, so she's quite unsuspecting when Jeanne and Mike offer to take her out to dinner the weekend before. I'm by the window, on the lookout, when Jeanne, Mike, and Sadie pull up to the restaurant. From where I am standing, I can see the joy on

Sadie's face as she makes her way up the long walkway to the restaurant. She loves coming to this particular restaurant, so before the festivities even begin, I know Jeanne has done extremely well. We quiet the mob, making sure Sadie is none the wiser as she nonchalantly walks in.

Almost instantaneously, as with a swarm of bees, Sadie is overtaken by more than a hundred people rushing toward the doorway. As her guests make various attempts to get closer, in order to say their hellos and happy birthdays, Sadie realizes she's looking at more than her children and grandchildren. There are cousins, nieces and nephews, some seventy or older and others much younger. Many of these relatives have come thousands of miles just to be here. Sadie can't believe it as she glances around the room, and an even bigger smile graces her face. Yet nothing lights up her smile more than the sight of her baby sister Angelina, sitting nearby in her wheelchair, happily watching the crowd while patiently waiting a turn to greet the big sister she loves so much.

Sadie looks absolutely smashing tonight in a perfectly-fitted black satin dress as she exudes pure joy. The change to reddish hair compliments her look nicely, and to no one's surprise, Sadie is the center of attention, and as fashionable as ever.

The time has come to reveal Sadie's other birthday surprise, so everyone steps aside to reveal her guest star— Tony Orlando!

—⟡ **Sadie's 90th Birthday Party** ⟡—
Sadie dancing with Tony Orlando at her party

I smile every time I think about that special night.

Sadie is a woman who positively impacts so many lives, and today their very presence touches her heart. Tony Orlando has been known to treat Sadie like a superstar whenever his manager and friend, Susan, brings her grandmother to see his shows in Florida or Atlantic City.

Sadie makes a point to tell Tony, the first time they meet that as much as she loves bingo, she loves him more; explaining how she had to quit bingo after the *Tony Orlando and Dawn* show changed nights. "I wasn't about to miss your show for anything in the world!" Tony was deeply touched by her devotion and decides to fly to New York to honor Sadie on her special day, to show his devotion; and he isn't going to miss this party for anything.

Just like her.

Whenever my daughter Susan and Sadie are in the same state, Susan makes it a point to see her Grandma Sadie, even if it's for a short while.

Susan happens to be in New York the same week Sadie is visiting, but Susan is heading back to Los Angeles that night, and doesn't want to miss the chance to see Sadie. But Sadie doesn't want to miss the chance to play bingo and asks Susan if she would mind picking her up at St. Vincent's Church. Susan heads out right after her last appointment to pick her up, but worries it might be difficult to find her grandmother in the overcrowded church-basement turned bingo hall, and wishes her Sadie would have skipped bingo.

When Susan rushes into the back of the crowded room, Sadie is easily spotted amidst the sea of silver haired women, her luscious black locks bringing your eyes right to her row. Sadie isn't even looking around to find Susan; she's too busy concentrating on her many cards and continues to nonchalantly play bingo in the second row center as Susan reaches the front. To Susan's great delight, minutes later someone else wins the game, and off they go.

I will never forget the day her husband, Jimmie passed away making Sadie a widow early in life, at only fifty-two-years-old. This afforded her the luxury to spend more time with all of us over the next forty years, but it was devastating for her. Fortunately, she was able to fulfill her travel dreams, going on many grand adventures later in life, yet even Sadie never expected at the age of eighty-five to travel to the State of Israel, to walk where Jesus walked.

To anyone asking about her newest adventure, she was heard saying in a convincingly sweet voice, "It's never too late to fulfill any of your lifelong dreams!"

Sadie does the things she loves to stay young, and she has a big place in her heart for television host, Pat Sajak. She's also an avid and delightfully neat search-a-word player who excels at *Wheel of Fortune*. In the morning she watches *The Price Is Right*, rarely missing a show, and is a major Bob Barker fan. Sadie derives happiness from all the aspects of life, but particularly enjoys homemade pasta eaten in a kitchen and thoroughly enjoys a cold beer with a slice of pizza. Her greatest joys have always been people, and the cherished relationships with those surrounding her on this extraordinary day—Sadie's 90th birthday.

Sadie is my very own Naomi from the Bible. After the burial of Naomi's son (Ruth's husband) she strongly suggests to Ruth that she should go back to the village of her own family, and that she'll be okay.

Ruth didn't listen, and stays with Naomi.

Jimmie and I were married for fifty-nine years, but had our circumstances been different, I would've followed Sadie, my mother-in-law, to the ends of the earth just to be near her. Because when someone as special as Sadie comes into your life, you know what you have to do.

Follow her.

PART VII

꩜ **Our Golden Anniversary ~ June 8, 1996** ꩜

True love lasts forever!

CHAPTER 17

Pearls of Wisdom

The weather is perfect on this eighth day of June, 1996.

Jimmie and I are walking up the cobblestone path leading to the glass door entrance to the most fabulous Italian restaurant this side of the Hudson. Inside, over ninety guests anxiously await our grand entrance. We feel like newlyweds again, all dressed up and smiling ear-to-ear, as Jimmie opens the door. He gently clutches my hand, and then quickly pulls me through the door, down the hallway and into the grand ballroom. He's dragging a plastic ball and chain, conveniently tied around his ankle. Our guests love it, and everyone is cracking up, including me.

It's our 50th wedding anniversary and the party has begun. I couldn't be happier. Sadie's ninetieth birthday celebration was a recent milestone in her life and this anniversary is our milestone, and she is here. The depth of joy and love surrounding us are hardly describable, but I'll do my best.

An elaborate five-course meal is being served, and in between the courses, many of our guests dance to classic Frank Sinatra songs and other party favorites. As soon as Sister Sledge's hit song, "We Are Family" begins to play, all of our daughter's quickly line up and begin to sing their theme, and dance back and forth as several enthusiastic guests dance around them amidst a background of mass chatter.

It's almost time for the cake, coffee, and Italian cookies. Everyone is asked to gather one last time in the grand ballroom as our daughters gather along the brick fireplace. At this moment, I am completely overwhelmed with pride as I watch my daughters ready their speeches, with joyful bright smiles. When I look over at Jimmie and Sadie, they're smiling with tremendous pride too.

Jimmie breaks the awkward silence by telling our guests jokes laced with various complaints about deserving a medal for putting up with fifty years of my many quirks.

My quirks, what about his?

His descriptions of—open cabinet doors, lights on in the whole house, or the nightly spraying of Windex on everything in sight—sometimes too close to leftovers and maybe in the faces of guests—leaves everyone laughing. Hey, I wanted to get it done, sit down in the living room, and relax like everybody else; yet I suppose he has a good point, and that as surely as my quirks drove him a little crazy, I'm absolutely sure he wouldn't trade in a moment.

Let the festivities begin! Each of our six daughters present one of the elaborately decorated medals; three of them for each of us. From oldest to our youngest, they give speeches that are warm, touching, and at times, incredibly funny. Our girls go about hitting the proverbial nails right on the head, and as James Anthony likes to say in full dramatics, "I'm feeling the full gamut of emotions." It's what we're all feeling at the moment. After the presentations, the guests find their way back to our elegantly decorated tables. The windows are suddenly lit with the setting sun whilst inviting the glorious green trees inside to relish in the rose-colored ambiance filling the room. When we sit down for the much-awaited desserts I turn my gaze toward the glistening Hudson River and see the photographer ready to capture the rest of our lasting memories.

I will not wait.

Tonight, I will bask in all the love and all of my blessings, and they are many. I thank God for the life I was given, and it's such a wonderful thing to be so aware of the moment, to feel such utter happiness inside. What happens next even I never expected, nor can I believe. As a wonderful dessert follows a fabulous dinner, my evening culminates in what for me is the icing on the cake. Sadie is sitting beside me, since my mother had passed away earlier that year, and she leans in to hand me a gift—the cultured pearls—my Jimmie sent to her while serving in the South Pacific.

Looking at the pearls resting softly in Sadie's hands, I say to myself, "These beautiful pearls must be for me?"

Sadie wants me to have the precious pearls sent by her son, who captured my heart; they are strung together beautifully with a delicate wispy golden clasp, as she motions for me to put them on. Almost simultaneously, we well-up, but with a little help, I have the pearls on. This is the most precious gift anyone could imagine. I can be seen clutching the securely-fastened pearls in the party photos, as if for no other reason than to hold onto that moment forever.

They say in heaven there are seven pearly gates and each glorious gate is made from one single pearl; each beyond beautiful with an almost unimaginable presence of its own. Within a few months after she gives me the pearls, Sadie passes through one of those pearly gates in her own deserved glory of beauty, love, and heavenly presence.

God gave us a magnificent gift in Sadie, and I'm grateful to be giving you *Sadie's Pearls*—a rare glimpse into the wisdom and life of a remarkable woman who like a treasured pearl—is never to be forgotten.

⟿ Receiving my Precious Pearls from Sadie ⟿
The precious pearl necklace Jimmie sent to Sadie during WWII

My Enlightenment

BY ANNE MARIE

While camping at the Edison Camp in Shaver Lake, California, the glorious pines reminded me of the scenery from Lake Taconic near my sister Jeanne's house.

That was the last summer I visited our mom, purportedly to work on the book, and where from the busy highway you'd never guess there was a lake with camping, boating, and lots of locals. But there it was and there we were, in bathing suits, sipping drinks and getting a tan; another one of Tina's favorite things to do.

During that leisurely hike around the trails at Camp Edison, Paul and I venture into their tiny library where I immediately take notice of the book, The Purpose Driven Life, by Rick Warren. Mom had given me a copy of the book several years ago, but I haven't read it yet, so I pick theirs up and begin flipping through its pages. Paul looks at me like what other purpose could you possibly need. I tell him this is the book that inspired mom to finish what she set out to do in 1995, and I was curious.

Granted, her writings started with the spiral notebook at Henry Mayo Hospital, but it was reading The Purpose Driven Life that convinces her to fulfill her dream. I carefully set their copy back on the shelf and say to Paul, "Wow, that book really works."

Mom was right, we're often led in ways we cannot fathom on our own and we really shouldn't fight it. I sometimes speak of things still as primarily fate or coincidence, though its meaning does include God's plan for me these days.

And there were a couple of specific times I was going to read The Purpose Driven Life, mostly after being greeted with Mom's continual enthusiasm and my waning hope that we'll ever finish. I have been telling myself, "You don't have the time to fulfill your purpose-driven life, you're too busy helping Mom fulfill hers." But with *Sadie's Pearls* all but polished up and possibly a bit more time on my hands, I'll read the book that inspired her.

Who knows what it could lead too next?

Our Charlotte house in
La Grangeville, NY

Anne Marie with
Grandma Sadie - 1996

At Capriccio's in New York
New Year's Day

Tina and Anne Marie
(her wedding Day) - 2005

Tina's Acknowledgements

To the Lord, I want to thank you for giving me the strength and courage to fulfill my dream to write Sadie's Pearls. I am blessed to see it come true.

For Sadie, the most magnificent mother-in-law a girl could ask for. Without the lifelong friendship we shared and your gentle wisdom, this book would never have been written to honor your lessons. Thank you.

For my husband Jimmie, thank you for fifty-nine wonderful years together, you were my sweetheart and will always be the love of my life.

To my mother and father, I am grateful for your love and lifelong commitment to our family.

To my terrific sisters, Mary and Jean, thank you for your optimism and always being there when I needed you most. To my cousin Francis; thanks for your genuine enthusiasm; caring ways and always treating me like a sister.

To my sister-in-law Carmela and my late sister-in-law Jeanne to whom I am forever grateful for our family memories, wonderful life blessings, and especially for your unwavering encouragement to write Sadie's Pearls.

To my brother-in-law, Mike and my sister-in-law, Marie and their other siblings who have gone before us; Sonny,

Theresa, Anthony, and Anna, and their spouses who have also passed, I thank you for your love, friendships and the terrific family times we've shared over the years.

Thanks to my nieces and nephews who've been there to support me, but especially to Anthony and Diane, Susan D, Gina, Angela and Dominic, and Angela and Jim, for always treating me so incredibly special. I love you all.

To Lori, you are a dear and loyal friend, and I thank you for your encouraging words over the years, and also for validating my big dream.

To cherished friends who have gone before me, Fran and Bob, thank you both for the many decades of loyal friendship and the terrific times we shared. To Lydia and Bill, I will always be grateful for our lasting friendship and the good times we enjoyed. To my dearest girlfriend, Bernice, I will always miss you, and remember I will love you more.

To my sons-in-law, Anthony, John, and Paul, my thanks, love and appreciation for treating me with the utmost respect and honor. To the honorary seventh sister, Terri, I cherish you for your spirit and deep love for me and your honorary sisters.

To my daughter Susan, the greatest gift a daughter can give her mother is to believe in her dreams. I love you and thank you for your unwavering faith and commitment to this project.

To my late-daughter Marie, I admired your inner strength and your ability to find joy even during the toughest times in life. You were certainly taken too soon and we all miss you dearly. I am thankful for your beautiful family. To James Anthony, his wife Samantha, and their daughter Gianna, to Neil and Diana, their son Jovani, and Neil's daughter Kristina, and his son Anthony; to Vincent, his wife Yurani and their children, Marie and Vincent; and to Michael, his wife Alexia, and their children, Vincent and Giselle.

The greatest admiration and love to my daughters: To Tina and her children: Christi Anne, Anthony, and James and his wife Shannon; to Jeanne and her children: Christine and John Michael, his wife Kaitlyn, and their son, John Vincent; and to Toni Ann and her son Stephen, I treasure and thank God for each and every one of you.

Most of all, I give my deepest gratitude to my daughter Anne Marie for her astonishing effort. I love you and thank you from the bottom of my heart for your admirable dedication, precious time, and talent in helping bring *Sadie's Pearls* to life! You made my dream come true.

Jimmie and Tina with our beautiful daughters~ 1998
Toni Ann, Jeanne, Susan, Anne Marie, Marie and Tina